Library of
Davidson College

At the Risk of
Idolatry

At the Risk of Idolatry

by Warren Carr

Judson Press · Valley Forge

AT THE RISK OF IDOLATRY

Copyright © 1972
Judson Press, Valley Forge, Pa. 19481

All rights reserved. No part of this publication may be reproduced, stored in a retrieval system, or transmitted in any form or by any means, electronic, mechanical, photocopying, recording, or otherwise, without the prior permission of the copyright owner, except for brief quotations included in a review of the book.

Library of Congress Cataloging in Publication Data

Carr, Warren.
  At the risk of idolatry.

  Includes bibliographical references.
  1. Church. 2. Institutionalism (Religion)
I. Title.
BV600.2.C338   262   72-75356
ISBN 0-8170-0564-1

Except where otherwise indicated, the Bible quotations in this volume are in accordance with the Revised Standard Version of the Bible, copyright © 1946 and 1954, by the Division of Christian Education of the National Council of the Churches of Christ in the United States of America, and are used by permission.

Printed in the U.S.A.

To the people of:
- The Red House Baptist Church, Richmond, Kentucky
- The Providence Baptist Church, Winchester, Kentucky
- The First Baptist Church, Coeburn, Virginia
- The First Baptist Church, Princeton, West Virginia
- The Watts Street Baptist Church, Durham, North Carolina
- The Wake Forest Baptist Church, Winston-Salem, North Carolina

I wish to express gratitude to Mrs. Uber Stanford for typing, correction, and generous interest; to Mr. Jack Bracey for reading the original manuscript in the rough; and to my wife, Martha, for allowing me the time and for assisting with details.

Contents

1. In Behalf of Churchmen 9

2. The Young Destroyers: Individualists 17

3. The Young Destroyers: Revolutionaries 28

4. Humanists 37

5. Unbiblical Churchmen 48

6. The Idolatrous Risk 56

7. The Sacred and the Profane 69

8. On Becoming a Sectarian Institution 82

9. The Need of a Dramatizing Presence 96

10. Toward Putting on a Good Show 106

11. In Need of a Servant Church 115

12. The Servant Church 126

Notes 142

1. In Behalf of Churchmen

This is a book in behalf of churchmen. I am determined to justify those who have stayed with the institutional church, although they wonder why and suffer strange feelings of guilt. Because they have endured, they deserve to know the reason why and to be relieved of whatever guilt they may feel.

The odds are not encouraging. To be in the church is now something less than the height of fashion. That Christians are whipping a dead horse in their race for glory is a common assumption. Even the most committed religious ear cannot avoid the news: the church is passing out irrelevance with a cunning equal to that of exchanging Confederate money. The religious scene reeks with irony. Many of us who have remained know the temptation to "bootleg" what little religion we may have left.

Times are ripe for initiating a "religions anonymous movement." A university co-ed offers a good example. She was angered because she had to take "religion" before she could graduate. She registered her displeasure by refusing to purchase an annotated Bible for a course in New Testament. This turned out to be a mistake in strategy. Anyone seeing her carrying her annotated Bible could have reasonably surmised that her religious pursuits were mostly academic.

But when she appeared with her ordinary-looking Bible, it was quite possible for her peers to misconstrue her religious interests. Her solution was a gem. For the rest of the semester she carried her "King James" across campus in a brown paper bag.

Although most churchmen will not go to such extremes, they do take considerable pains to disguise their religious status. Their means of remaining incognito are many and varied. All have the same purpose, and that is to make sure that others are surprised to discover that they are Christian. Such a tendency must be turned around and as soon as possible. Let it be said immediately, however, that I hold no brief for those who are supinely comfortable under their ecclesiastical umbrellas. They are not to be commended for taking cover when the "heat is on." To live at "ease in Zion" in days like these could mean that the church is not taken seriously enough to be criticized. No honest churchman will refuse to rap the church when it deserves it.

Perhaps this is the best place for me to make my own confession. I have not always been happy in the church and am not now in all respects. I have experienced the same wonder and guilt that has bothered my fellow Christians. Clergymen are finding it just as difficult to stay with the church as are the laymen. Many of my professional colleagues have already made their exits. More are planning to do the same thing. The exodus shows no signs of abating in the near future. Many of my fellow clergymen explain that they are leaving in search of wider and more relevant ministries. That does not enhance my self-image. If their departure promises more relevance, does not my staying indicate less relevance?

Nevertheless, I have stayed. Nevertheless, I intend to stay.

Among other reasons, some good and some bad, laymen are a main cause for my remaining. When I first heard that God was dead, according to Nietzsche, I was too young to know one way or another. I kept on going to church. No one provided an incontrovertible rebuttal to Nietzsche's premise. After all, I am afraid that most preachers had never heard of Nietzsche in those days. Fewer still could spell his name. I went to church out of habit. I went because there was nowhere else to go. And I went because my parents did not know anything about Nietzsche either and cared less.

In retrospect I hope I may have intuited, albeit dimly, what Rudolf Bultmann would later put on paper:

> True Christian preaching is . . . a proclamation which claims to be the call of God through the mouth of man and, as the word of authority, demands belief. It is its characteristic paradox that in it we meet *God's* call in *human* words.[1]

As it turned out, I am sure that I heard some human words about a living God to put against Nietzsche's human words about a dead one.

After a number of years some human voices in the church decided that Nietzsche had been correct. This marked the beginning of the "death of God" theology. As the doctrine gained momentum, its advocates led the way in a modern exodus from the church.

I stayed. I stayed out of habit. I stayed because there was nowhere else to go. I stayed as well to hear some contemporary human voices proclaiming a living God.

As it turned out, the affirmation for which I was waiting came from unexpected sources. It did not come by way of brilliant argument against the doctrine of divine death. It was not shouted down by more vigorous and penetrating theological sounds. In a most remarkable way the rise and decline of the "death of God epic" was marked by the stubborn faith and practice of the laity. Radical theology more than met its match in the laymen, and they are chiefly responsible for its demise.

The actions of so many of us clergymen at that time are still an embarrassment to me. I was as guilty as the rest. Of course, we assured our congregations that God was in very good health. I do not think that we were very convincing. How could we have been when we so clearly revealed our own panic? We were provoked when laymen kept coming to worship, serving on committees, enjoying fellowship, and setting Communion for the Holy Presence as if nothing were changed. We even chided them for being the kind of churchmen who would go on "playing church" even if they discovered that God indeed were dead.

Our homiletic harangues were to no avail. The laymen hung on to the most immediate symbol they knew — the church. Could there have been a providential realization on their part? Did they know that radical theology would soon collapse because it had no immediate and lasting symbol of its own? Who can say? One thing is sure: There can be no church of a dead or a dying God. There can only be the "church of the living God."

In all probability these laymen did not know the reasons for their persistence. It would have helped had they been able to express their motives clearly and abundantly. This may have made our connections with the church less tentative than they are. Be that as it may, it was the faithful laymen rather than the clergy who brought us through a trying time.

I must ask: where are those laymen now? It would be gratifying if it were possible to sign off sounding their praises. That is not possible. Perhaps the battle has exhausted them. Whatever the reason, they are no longer around in the same numbers and with the same undaunted spirit. Let us hope that they are not a vanishing breed already beyond the point of recovery. In any event I can do no less for them than they did for me. As they have helped me to affirm and love the church, so now I am constrained to do as much for them.

Such a mission will demand a radical statement. Do not be misled by the mellow tones I have used up to this point. I am well aware that there is nothing radical about affirming the church. But there can be considerable risk in affirming it as an institution. I dare to commend the church because it is an institution rather than despite that fact.

Far more eloquent and powerful voices than mine are

taking an opposite point of view. If and when they trouble with church reform, they make elaborate plans to purge it of its institutional blight. They must not prevail. The end of the religious institution could mean the end of faith.

DEFINITION AND DESCRIPTION

Now is the time to define what I think has been grossly victimized and which I hasten to defend. As I see it, institution in the broadest sense — its very idea and purpose — has been summoned to a kangaroo court. It is the target of irresponsible indictments. It is under duress for being what it has to be by virtue of its own character.

According to the dictionary an institute or institution may be a number of things. For the purpose at hand its most suitable definition is an "organization for the promotion of a cause."

Causes cannot be promoted unless they are made visible by the organization that supports them. Institutions bring causes out of hiding. They can no longer be secret. In like respect institutions identify people with causes. They incarnate human intentions. Form and substance are given to human values. An institution tends to program a person's faith. By so doing, it strongly insinuates that a faith worth having is a faith worth programming.

Obviously, any person is more effectively bound to whatever cause he institutionalizes. He cannot privately defect from such a cause. If he wishes to forsake it, he must also withdraw from the organization which has given it public meaning and status. Furthermore, if he does not withdraw, the institution may drag him along in the process of promoting the cause which he began. Once any organization is formed to promote a mission, it is not easily deterred by fickle people whose love grows cold with facility. Institutions are more consistent in their commitment to causes than are the people who embraced those causes in the first place.

The institution's penchant for persistence is what Carl Gustavson has called the "institutional drive." This is the very characteristic which draws the greatest wrath from the critics. In reference to this drive Gustavson has written:

> In sum this refers to the tendency of any organization, associational or state, to intensify control over its membership while also reaching outward to strengthen its position in the environment. . . . Inherent in any situation where men are joined in group enterprises, it is a sociological phenomenon both necessary and dangerous.[2]

If it were not for the whimsical nature of man, institutional drive would not be a matter of necessity. As it stands, however, the success of causes is dependent upon institutions in the long run. Unless people are organized, they do not substantiate their visions. The institution of marriage is a good illustration. Marriage counselors of every ilk know that they must start with disaffected couples where they are when they come for help. Most of these couples seek counsel for the purpose of saving their marriage. This is where the counseling must begin although that is not where it should remain. But the point can be made that husbands and wives often seek help because their marriages are institutions commanding their long-term commitment.

Because of this element of necessity, institutional drive is all the more dangerous. The danger point is not reached when an institution perpetuates itself by modifying the purposes for which it was designed. Changes of this kind are often vital and effective. The danger peaks when an institution becomes concerned with nothing but its own perpetuation and when it will sacrifice its integrity and its mission for that purpose.

This is the dilemma. Without its tendency for self-perpetuation, an institution can hardly endure the ordeals of opposition and neglect. Because of this tendency, institutions do distort and controvert the purposes for which they presumably exist. They usually begin in the womb of high idealism. They are often envisioned as vehicles of limitless possibilities. The family is interpreted as a treasure house of love, fidelity, and wholesome nurture. Schools represent bridges to the truth which makes men free. Business is meant to insure happiness and prosperity for all men. Government promises an ordered and tranquil society of, by, and for the people. The church is an agent of redemption — the salt of the earth and the light of the world.

When these organizations fail their mission and come short of such lofty ideals, the frenzy of anti-institutionalism should come as no surprise. Unless a balance between the necessity and the danger of the institutional drive is achieved, the frenzy will continue.

A secondary purpose of this book, yet an important one, is to call for a sane approach to the institutional problem. Jerome Skolnick and Elliot Currie contend that American scholars have largely abdicated the function of institutional criticism. In the vacuum, created by a lack of appropriate study, frenetic condemnation of institutions has taken up its residence. There can be no doubt that the social changes called for in these times cannot be accomplished without functioning institutions. In that light, the institutional problem cannot be ignored. Skolnick and Currie contend:

> ... focusing on institutional problems has to do with values ... appropriate to a democratic society. Democratic conceptions of society have always held that institutions exist to serve man, and that, therefore, they must be accountable to men. Where they fail to meet the tests imposed on them, democratic theory holds that they ought to be changed. Authoritarian governments, religious regimes, and reformatories, among other social systems, hold the opposite: in case of misalignment between the individuals or groups and the "system," the individuals or groups are to be changed or to otherwise be made unproblematic. Somewhere between these conceptions lies the working ideology of conventional social problems theory.[3]

That the religious institution is not a lonely and isolated target is evident. Institutions are generally in trouble. Although the church may not like its place alongside authoritarian governments and reformatories, it is in the category which does not quickly comply with man's attempts to change it when it no longer serves him as he wishes. If Skolnick and Currie are right, then the church is indispensable to provide the balance of which I have spoken.

The survival of the major institutions of the West is

presently at stake. The opposition is highly motivated and well equipped. Institutions can no longer delay their responsibility for talking back to their critics. No institution is better prepared than the church to initiate the dialogue. I hope that this retort, at the very least, will encourage similar ones before it is too late.

2. The Young Destroyers: Individualists

More vocal and visible than most other enemies of institutions are the young destroyers. They believe in taking direct and overt action until the institutions are destroyed. Theodore Roszak has measured and explained their disaffection in *The Making of a Counter Culture*. He is convinced that this generation has lost control of the institutions which have formerly shaped its culture. It is mainly an adult hand which has lost its grip. As a result, America's youth have begun to wage an undeclared war on the establishment.

Roszak evaluates the situation with a mixture of hope and regret:

> Unlike their parents, who must kowtow to the organizations from which they win their bread, the youngsters can talk back at home with little fear of being thrown out in the cold. One of the pathetic, but, now we see, promising characteristics of postwar America has been the uppityness of adolescents and the concomitant reduction of the paterfamilias to the general ineffectuality of a Dagwood Bumstead. In every family comedy of the last twenty years, dad has been the buffoon.[1]

The author's vested hope in uppity adolescents is generally compatible with the modern mood. "Dad—the buffoon" is thought to be a well-deserved epithet. In a manner akin to the father's loss of control of the family constellation, so have adults let other institutions take the bit in their teeth and run wild. Youth have decided that stronger and more intelligent hands are needed at the reins. But in their terrible anger they are more likely to wind up killing the horse.

The prospect is grim. Massive bungling by their elders has left the greater burden of dissent on the strong but erratic shoulders of the youngsters. It is a hectic situation comprised of a majority of cowed adults, too frightened to resist the institutions which have become their "Frankensteins," and a mob of courageous young people, too immature and unskilled to remedy the condition. Roszak confesses:

> It is not ideal, it is probably not even good that the young should bear so great a responsibility for inventing or initiating for their society as a whole. It is too big a job for them to do successfully. It is indeed tragic that in a crisis that demands the tact and wisdom of maturity, everything that looks most hopeful in our culture should be building from scratch—as must be the case when the builders are absolute beginners.[2]

Yet another pessimism may be added to Roszak's gloomy pile. There is no guarantee that young people are committed to building a counter culture. Their skill is not the only factor in doubt. Dedication to any kind of culture hangs on a giant question mark as far as they are concerned.

A PREMIUM ON INDIVIDUALITY

The average youngster may have already reckoned the percentage against his "inventing or initiating for [his] society as a whole." The slant of the odds may have caused him to lose interest. Perhaps this explains why he now places a fantastic premium upon his own individuality. Having witnessed what uncontrolled and voracious institutions have done to his human antecedents, he no longer aspires to build a society or even a counter culture. His main concern is to build up himself. And he has apparently concluded that this is impossible as long as existing institutions hold sway over the people. Because these institutions apparently destroyed the personal individuality of his forbears, he sees no recourse but to topple them if he is to realize his own selfhood.

So widespread and intense is this youthful temperament that a marriage between extant institutions and today's youngsters is almost out of the question. Individualism is a highly attractive and seductive mistress persuading most young people to make no new covenants with the establishment and to break those which have already been made.

Responsible individualism is not incompatible with institutions. Unfortunately, this is not the kind of individualism which has captured the fancy of youth. If Reinhold Niebuhr is analytically accurate, today's young people "dig" Renaissance mentality and are negative to that of the Reformation. Niebuhr minces no words:

> If Protestantism represents the final heightening of . . . the Christian religion, the Renaissance is the real cradle of that very unchristian concept and reality: the autonomous individual. . . .
> The nexus between the Christian and the Renaissance individual is not the Protestant idea of the individual's sole responsibility to God but the medieval mystical idea of the infinite potentialities of the human spirit.[3]

"The infinite potentiality of the human spirit" speaks to our new breed of "Renaissance youth," who are quickly convinced as to the unlimited possibilities of themselves. As they see the situation, the main barrier to self-realization is the establishment. It is therefore obvious that the establishment must give way under the trampling of their pilgrim feet.

CHARACTERISTICS OF AUTONOMOUS INDIVIDUALISM

One major characteristic of autonomous individualism is that it depends more on essence than upon distinctiveness. An autonomous individual thinks of *being* rather than of being different. He expects to become an individual when he is able to know himself, and he scrutinizes that self in isolation rather than in community. Knowing and becoming himself is his goal. He cares little about his distinctiveness within the whole, which is more the mark of a responsible individual.

Some years ago, I received a delightful postcard cartoon

that was making the rounds. Its background was a theater filled to capacity. A sentimental episode on the screen had reduced the vast audience to tears. There was a notable exception. One man in the very center of the crowd was doubled up with laughter. Beneath the scene was this caption: "A man who thinks for himself."

Responsible individuals, conscious of being distinguishable from the mass, think *for themselves*. Autonomous individuals, conscious of their own essence, think *of themselves*. It would be unfair to claim that the latter have no sense of responsibility. They do have but it usually turns inward. If they saw individuality as a matter of distinctiveness, their sense of responsibility would encompass the wider community. This would include society and its institutions.

Young destroyers do not cotton to concepts of this kind. They confirm Kenneth Cauthen's observations:

> The spirit of our age is infused with the assumption that meaning must be humanly created, that truth is relative, that values are subjective and that the universe doesn't give a damn what we do or believe. . . .
> The secular mind assumes that man is responsible for his own destiny, hence for directing the course of history toward goals of his own choosing.[4]

Obviously, young and autonomous individualists, pursuing the goals of their decisions, are leery of all social agents which incline toward mutual decisions about such goals. No agent is more likely to get in their way than is the institution. It has very little interest in or tolerance for the person who "does his own thing."

It is almost impossible for a person to know himself or to live autonomously within an institution. He is constantly reminded of others, of the demands of the institution, and of his obligation to society. In a word, individuals may find their distinctiveness within institutions but are not likely to find a pristine essence, which seems to be the chief desire of autonomous individuals.

A recall of a graduation gift from my father illustrates another major characteristic of autonomous individuals. With a wristwatch he gave me was appended this note: "In time and on time are two of the most important things in life. Do not forget either one of them." Responsibility demands that each of us honors the requirements of being in time and on time. But autonomous individuals prefer to ignore the restrictions of both time and place. These dimensions represent commitment to an external world which such people will avoid at all costs. It is more than coincidence that institutions are dependent upon time and place factors. They cannot exist without either of them. Institutions must run on schedule. Instead of being mobile, they are fixed as far as place is concerned.

The church is greatly resented because it must be subject to the demands of time and place. Its critics find a vulnerable spot with the reminder that God was more comfortable in a tent than in a temple. That the Scriptures condemn all attempts to domesticate God and pin him down to worldly structures cannot be denied. At the same time, to whatever extent the church is an institution, it cannot ignore time and place restrictions. To do otherwise would make it so capricious that it could not be dependable.

In innocent childhood we used to believe that the church was a *place* where you go to worship God *on Sunday*. At the very least we understood that the church was a *place* which operated *on time*. More sophisticated and "enlightened" arguments that the church is not a place and that it need not serve the time dimension are not convincing. Contrary to what might be supposed, the conceptions of our childhood never really contributed to the domestication of God. Classic worship has always invoked His particular Presence at some time and place. As long as the worship of God is not exclusively confined to these ecclesiastical dimensions, we need not shy away from the idea that "church is a place where you go to worship God on Sunday." That is far better than going to church with no more assurance than that God might possibly drop in. The childish version gains by the comparison.

Our youngsters will not agree. For the sake of their autonomous individuality, they would de-institutionalize the church by freeing it from restrictive factors of this kind. As chairman of a university chapel committee, I was introduced to this aversion more than once.

On one occasion, a student, who was to be in charge of one of the services, decided that the university's devotional chapel was not suitable for his purposes. He asked about the possibility of getting out of that "suffocating tomb and holding the service under a tree." Although I had no objection, I asked what tree he had in mind. Such information was necessary since I was responsible for publicizing the chapel services as to time and place.

The student was so upset by my question as to respond in anger. "That's the trouble with you and your crowd," he said, "you always have to pin down everything." In all honesty, I was not trying to hinder his plans. I did not relish the prospect, to be sure, of a canine exercise of sniffing out just the proper tree for the occasion. I never got an answer. With evident disgust he resorted to using the conventional meeting place in the university chapel.

Another time, in that same chapel, I saw an earnest young man bang his fist on its marble altar with mixed anger and frustration. Condemning it because it was fixed, immobile, and static, he made an impassioned plea for the church to move out into the world and get with the action. His presentation left me feeling accused and guilty. After some time for reflection, my attitude changed. I sought him out for conversation. Agreeing with him that the altar was quite immovable, I countered that the cross it supported was mobile and that he could shoulder it and carry it wherever he felt compelled. I also reminded him that should he ever decide to hang on a cross, it would have to be planted in something firm enough to hold the weight of his sacrifice. I cannot help but believe that this is what altars are really all about.

Neither of these encounters was fruitful. The minds of these young men were not changed. My mind was not changed. Having protected their individuality from the stereotypical voice of the establishment, they walked away. As they departed, I jumped to a regrettable conclusion of my own. I felt unhappily certain that if they were ever asked to choose between walking in the steps of Christ or Christ walking in the steps of them, Christ would have to be the One who followed.

THE FAMILY

Although autonomous individuals augur ill for every institution, the family bears the brunt of their destructive disfavor. It could hardly be any other way. The family is the essence of corporateness and of responsible individualism. Modern youth spend much time and great ingenuity in getting away from both.

The maturation of children demands their growing away from the initial parasitic dependence of the fetus upon the mother. This process moves inexorably toward the time when the adolescent begins his final break with the family. So far as we know, there is no better way to grow up. The drive for independence is a necessary element in any pilgrimage toward a healthy maturity. Independence is not, however, completely synonymous with genuine and ultimate maturity. The mature person recognizes the importance of interdependence. Only an adolescent mentality preaches that a mature person needs no one. The mature mind tutors more sensibly than this. Man reaches his maturation when he recognizes his need of others and their need of him.

It took much time and many events for Elijah to learn this lesson. At one time, he took on an entire company of Baal's prophets in splendid isolation. (Cf. 1 Kings 18:17-40.) It was strictly a one-man show. God was exceptionally kind to Elijah. I have long thought that it would have served the prophet right if the Lord had left him standing alone on his mountain with all that wet wood in his hands.

Even after Jezebel sent him scurrying, Elijah stuck with the pose of an autonomous individual. He claimed to be the only one in Israel who had not bowed down before Baal. When Yahweh finally ran Elijah down in his hideout, the Lord pointed out that at least seven thousand other people had never bent a knee to Baal. (Cf. 1 Kings 19:9-18.)

As a necessary modification of complete independence, interdependence indicates that no man can exist without using resources other than his own. Youthful autonomists do not like the sound of that. Because they need financial support as well as more intangible forms of care, they live in somewhat of a bind. Some of them think that they have handled the contradiction if they never ask for help. This is no more than a presumption upon parental grace. But they persist in neither asking nor expressing gratitude for help as a proof of their independence.

Interdependence also entails responsibility. Children tend to envy parents because of the latter's seeming freedom from having to ask them for anything. It is true that a family tilts to one side on this matter. Children must depend on their parents who need not depend on them. This is not the real sign of parental maturity no matter what the children may think. Mature parents are marked by responsibility more than by independence. No family could survive the chaos of parents who are independent without being responsible.

Both interdependence and responsibility are necessary to the institution of the family. In no way does this combination outlaw individuality of the proper kind. Unless each member of it is a distinguishable individual, the family cannot reach its potential any more than its separate members are able to do. But this means responsible individualism rather than the autonomous brand.

Responsibility in the context of interdependence takes on the nature of corporate responsibility. Even so, it does not unconditionally replace the responsibility of the person. Corporate responsibility receives much less than *carte blanche* approval from the Scriptures.

Ezekiel, and Jeremiah as well, posed opposition to the

idea of corporate responsibility in their rhetorical question to the exiles:

> What do you mean by repeating this proverb concerning the land of Israel, "The fathers have eaten sour grapes and the children's teeth are set on edge?" As I live, says the Lord God, this proverb shall no more be used by you in Israel. . . . Yet you say, "Why should not the son suffer for the iniquity of the father?" When the son has done what is lawful and right, and has been careful to observe all my statutes, he shall surely live. The soul that sins shall die. The son shall not suffer for the iniquity of the father, nor the father suffer for the iniquity of the son; the righteousness of the righteous shall be upon himself, and the wickedness of the wicked shall be upon himself (Ezekiel 18:2-3, 19-20; cf. Jeremiah 31:29-30).

The suggestion of autonomous and rugged individualism is certainly here, but the prophets were emphasizing the responsibility of each individual. Under the same set of circumstances, their message would be just as appropriate now as it was then. The prophets were addressing the exiles and probably the younger leaders of a distressed people in particular. In their unhappy plight, these leaders were opting for corporate responsibility in preference to responsible individualism.

They dusted off an ancient proverb with which to finger their elders and forefathers as being chiefly responsible for their unbearable situation. The proverb may have found its clue in Exodus law (Exodus 20:5b): ". . . for I the Lord your God am a jealous God, visiting the iniquity of the fathers upon the children to the third and fourth generation of those who hate me. . . ." In any event, Ezekiel warned them to put that proverb and its implications aside. He insisted that each exile must bear some responsibility for his own condition and act accordingly.

There are intriguing undertones to the narrative. Ezekiel's rebuke may have set the stage for the subsequent practice of Corban, consecrating gifts to God, which Jesus severely condemned in his time. Affinity between Corban and autonomous individualism appears to be a natural connection. It need not be contrived.

All of the contributing factors inhere in the story. We

know that exilic duress revived Israel's interest in the law of Moses. We can imagine with what emotions younger exiles heard the daily recital of the Decalogue from the lips of the elders, especially with reference to the unfulfilled promise of the Fifth Commandment: "Honor your father and your mother, *that your days may be long in the land* which the Lord your God gives you" (Exodus 20:12, italics added). It had not turned out like that at all. Presumably they had heeded that commandment as they carved out their future in the God-given land of promise. How great their rancor must have been when that promise was inexpressibly shattered!

The Pharisees were most instrumental in the renewed concern with the Law. There is no reason to believe, however, that they responded any differently to its recital than their exiled contemporaries. Is it possible that the younger element of Pharisaism developed the principle of Corban as a lawful circumvention of the Fifth Commandment? The idea did not surface in Jewish thought until after the Exile. In recording his indignation with the practice, Jesus addressed himself to the Pharisees:

> ... "You have a fine way of rejecting the commandment of God, in order to keep your tradition! For Moses said, 'Honor your father and your mother'; and, 'He who speaks evil of father or mother, let him surely die'; but you say, 'If a man tells his father or his mother, What you would have gained from me is Corban' (that is, given to God)—then you no longer permit him to do anything for his father or mother, thus making void the word of God through your tradition which you hand on . . ." (Mark 7:9-11).

So it was that a son or daughter made God his excuse for rejecting his parents. A son or daughter could thereby become autonomous.

The picture is not without coherence. Ezekiel and Jeremiah would not let the younger exiles hide behind corporate responsibility—the sins of the fathers—as the primary reason for being among the exiles. They contended that each person should accept individual responsibility for his misfortune and as the means by which he might effectively deal with it. If I am right about the possible emergence of Corban from this epoch, then it does follow that some of the Jewish leaders rejected the prophet's call for responsible individualism. They replaced it with individual autonomy. That concept is decidedly explicit in the posture and practice of Corban.

Similarity between the disillusioned youth of present times and their counterparts in exilic Judaism is unmistakable. If the concept of corporate responsibility does not indict modern parents for today's miserable situation, it does not commend itself to young people as being of any use. Embittered as they are, youth are disinclined to embrace the idea of individual responsibility. Not only would that burden them with a portion of the blame for contemporary social evils, but it would also make them partially responsible for pulling their elders out of the mire. Individuals they are willing to be — even eager to be — but they respond only to the pull of autonomous individualism. If this becomes sufficiently entrenched over the long haul, no institution can afford to take an easy breath; and the family, in particular, faces a disastrous future.

3. The Young Destroyers: Revolutionaries

While some of the "young destroyers" are preoccupied with becoming autonomous individuals at the expense of institutions, a small but foreboding minority is in a revolutionary mood. All too many times that mood erupts and spills over into violence and destruction.

The institution of the family has little to fear from the proponents of revolution. Their main targets are the institutions of government and education. Business would be given more prominent mention were it not for the fact that government is legally committed to protecting the rights of business and its property. As a consequence, when revolutionaries threaten the destruction of business, they usually wind up in a confrontation with the forces of government at one level or another. The same holds true for the schools but in a lesser degree, because most schools prefer to forgo governmental intervention except in the most extreme circumstances.

By its very nature, revolution begins with the impotent who are striving for power. It need not look for recruits from the power structure. That would be generally fruitless. Revolution attracts those who have been depressed by social, economic, and political powerlessness. And it must be admitted that institutional power blocs do not readily open their doors to the powerless masses. In all probability there is no such entity as a revolutionary institution. Some institutions are initially organized in order to accomplish revolutionary goals. As soon as they achieve a modicum of power, they are tempered with the flavor of unimpassioned compromise. If they wish to retain the power they have acquired, no other recourse seems possible for them. Even at its weakest stage, unless it is extremely ephemeral, almost any institution enjoys enough power to relish the idea of keeping it. Not only does it guard against any revolution which might attempt to disarm it by force, but it also has an equally watchful eye out for anyone who might slyly embezzle its strength. However necessary and noble they may be, institutions incessantly court their own corruption in their extraordinary lust for power.

The unassailable reality of this institutional characteristic fans the flame of revolution into uncompromising heat. Once revolution begins, it exploits human emotions as much as it can. It demands impassioned and irrational loyalty. It is both easier and safer to resign from an institution than from a revolution. Anyone leaving a revolution in midstream had better know how to swim or to walk on water. Otherwise, he may not make it to shore.

Young revolutionary destroyers thrive on the conviction that government has contributed more than its fair share to the fundamental malignancies of our society. For example, they bitterly resent a system which drafts young men to defend the "American way of life," when so many of them have never tasted its benefits. In their view, the American way is to run down its youth for military service, when it fails to search them out successfully for the purpose of rescuing them from poverty and cultural deprivation. Business and commercial enterprises have compounded the incongruity of this situation. They have made the good life televisionally familiar to masses of people for whom it can never be experientially familiar.

Young revolutionists resent racism in the land of the

free. They are outraged at a generation of profit-crazed polluters. They cannot tolerate the possibility that personal freedom and privatism are being "bugged" out of existence by intelligence units at both local and national levels.

They are especially cynical about their democratic right to freedom of speech. Until they are somehow granted the *right to be heard,* the right to free speech is of little consequence. Even our free society is not legally equipped for guaranteeing the right to be heard. Furthermore, in ways that are perfectly legal, most power structures are equipped with highly selective antennae. Whatever voices they want to hear receive immediate and rapt attention. Second on the list of priorities are voices which they do not want to hear but are afraid to tune out. Farthest down the list — almost out of sight — are voices so weak that they cannot demand a hearing. Each of these categories is free to speak. But it remains with the power structures to determine which ones will be heard.

Against that kind of powerful opposition, a revolutionary must make himself heard by whatever means possible. He has discovered that overt forms of violence are most likely to get a hearing. He knows that institutions cannot exist without the rights to property. Nor do institutions have either a present or a future except under the umbrella of law and order. In the light of what has already been said with respect to time and place, it is quite apparent that institutions are inextricably connected to both dimensions. Such realizations have helped to fashion the modern revolutionary's distinction between property rights and human rights. Because institutions are powerful and because they are dependent upon property, law and order, and time and place; revolution has adopted the tactic of destroying property, making a shambles of law and order, and upsetting the balance of time and place. As long as they move against institutions and their basic connections, they believe that they are acting under ethical sanctions. I believe that few of today's young firebrands are deliberate in their destruction of human beings. For the most part, this is accidental genocide. As long as they attack property rather than persons, they are able to feel moral about the whole business. Therein lies the reason that modern revolutions pose a greater threat to institutions than may have been the case in former years. It is a harsh truth that institutions are able to replace persons with greater facility than they can replace property or order.

Once these young revolutionaries have contrived to distinguish between property rights and human rights, they tend to violate property with reckless abandon. As an example, I recently witnessed a small altercation in the university cafeteria. One student took a belligerent swing at another. Cooler heads quickly separated the two and no great damage was done. Subsequently, the young man who had barely escaped having his head knocked off came over to our table. In answering someone's question about the cause of the dispute, he replied, "Oh, that guy is still hung-up on some 'high-schoolish' notion of property rights. I took something belonging to him without asking and he took offense. I just can't understand people like that."

As long as revolutionaries are convinced that human rights are sacrosanct while property rights are fair game, the bombing, burning, and usurpation of institutional property will continue. Laws prohibiting such deeds will consistently be treated as unjust. Thus law and order will also be mainstream targets before the revolutionary wrath.

REVOLUTION ON THE CAMPUS

Campus disruption is of the same stripe but with its own unique *raison d'etre*. It is assumed that no student can be honest and creative within the educational framework of law and order. This explains in part the unswerving efforts to reduce or eliminate the power of educational authorities.

The fact that students have perennially broken the laws of colleges and universities must not obscure the realities inherent in the present situation. The institutions are well prepared to deal with the ordinary kind of lawbreaking. As a matter of fact, most of their laws are designed to assure an ordered community as well as to present a proper image to their constituency. However, even those rules which are apparently designed for governing the personal morality of an individual are actually intent upon protecting the institution's social image.

As a consequence, most of these institutions make no more than token effort to uncover individual infractions as long as they are not discredited by them before the public. Campus security forces are not usually adept at wiretapping. Neither do they accumulate intricate files of intelligence data. All of this is to say that, as a general rule, students compound their crimes by getting caught. From the administration's point of view, students should not commit the sin of getting caught. The subsequent embarrassment suffered by the institution becomes the major issue.

Revolutionary students will no longer play this game. Under the guise of extreme aversion to all forms of hypocrisy, they insist on breaking laws in full public view. Their honesty cannot be denied, but it reaches the extreme of brutal honesty. Their prime aim is to embarrass the institution. They know that no university or college can tolerate this condition. It loses financial support whenever it suffers a bad image. Sometimes it is forced to shut down and go out of business.

Undoubtedly some of my readers are shocked by what seems to be my easy-going response to the hypocrisy of educational institutions. And I am sure that university administrators will resent its implications. Quite probably, however, their chief concern will be, "What will people think if they believe this to be true of us?" In that case, nothing more is needed to prove the point.

Although I hold no brief for brazen hypocrisy, the posture and practice of most universities in this context are to be commended rather than criticized. In no way does their hypocrisy merit or justify the destructive intentions of revolutionaries. Granted that educational institutions do not rigidly enforce their rules on personal morality, mainly for their own sakes, this by no means rules out the possibility that students benefit from the practice as well.

Dr. C. Macfie Campbell's witty aphorism, as quoted by Rollo May, is a delightful eye-opener. Dealing with the philosophical aspects of psychoanalysis, Dr. Campbell remarked: "Psychoanalysis is Calvinism in Bermuda shorts."[1] Perhaps we may update his observation and modify it at the same time: "Psychoanalysts are Calvinists in 'hot pants.'"

This is but to say that there is a strong strand of Puritanism in university officials, as well as in psychiatrists, no matter at what level of sophistication they may appear. As Puritans they affirm the necessity of social restraint by means of laws and regulations. As modern men they cannot ignore the unquestioned appeal and good sense in "situation ethics." In their realm, however, they cannot responsibly allow situation ethics to dominate completely the campus situation. Proponents of this ethic system persuasively argue that no law is consistently applicable and just, with respect to every circumstance. Trouble occurs when this fact is employed to undergird the supposition that laws are therefore generally useless.

Universities have always been able to function in the context of law-breaking. This is not the same condition as lawlessness. No institution can survive the complete absence of law. Although educational institutions must establish laws for the sake of their own existence, students are better served by lawful structures, even if they break their laws, than is the case with no law at all.

Rollo May has adroitly made this point. He writes:

> College students, in their fights with college authorities about hours girls are to be permitted in men's rooms, are curiously blind to the fact that rules are often a boon. Rules give the student time to find himself. He has the leeway to consider a way of behaving without being committed before he is ready, to try on for size, to venture into relationships tentatively—which is part of any growing up. . . . He may flaunt the rules; but at least they give some structure to be flaunted.[2]

The revolutionary aim on most contemporary campuses is not a campaign of breaking the rules in order to spotlight their injustice. It is a campaign for an atmosphere of lawlessness, a situation in which there are no laws remaining which ought to be broken. Were this to come to pass, no college or university could face the future without utter consternation.

REVOLUTIONARY CREATIVITY

One of the most subtle controversies of all springs out of the revolutionary's commitment to chaos as the essential element to creativity. Order, the opposite of chaos, is deemed to be a hindrance to creativity. As the revolutionary sees it, complete freedom to the point of anarchy is the most favorable atmosphere for genuine creativity.

The point is not to be ignored. Although by no means unanimous, there are convincing philosophical and theological agreements that God alone creates *ex nihilo* — out of nothing. This position, writes Langdon Gilkey, has "specifically denied the pre-existent matter, the finite God, and the necessary evil of dualism." [3]

Since this kind of creativity is possible by the power of God only, all human creativity necessarily is confined to giving form to substance and bringing order to chaos. Gilkey elaborates:

> When he makes something, or "creates" a work of art, man shapes in a new way some stuff, be it wood, stone, clay, paint or musical notes. His activity is genuinely creative; but his work presupposes a given material to be reworked, and even given forms, either from nature or from his imaginative experience of nature, which are regrouped. For human beings "to create" means to impose upon a given material a form it had not possessed before. It never can mean to produce either the material itself or all relevant forms.[4]

Our social institutions are poised for creativity of this kind. They exist in a highly complex society by virtue of advanced technology. This means that they are already highly ordered organizations which demand the genius of imagination if creative works are to ensue within their boundaries. The same may be said for society as a whole. Its civilized order challenges the resources of great imagination and ingenuity.

Young people face no more exciting prospect than that of being creative in a social order that borders on a technocracy. Educational institutions cannot avoid their responsibility for equipping their students to tackle even that large an order. As government beckons a greater participation by the young in its structure and function, it must keep this particular challenge in mind. Whatever contribution this may mean for our young people may be combined with the virtue of survival as far as these and the rest of the social institutions are concerned.

Such endeavors, however, are becoming increasingly difficult to get started. Our youngsters may be taking an easier way out. They are intrigued with bringing simplism and even primitivism to present-day society. There is a very good reason for doing so. It is so much easier to be creative in a simple and primitive environment. The more ordered and formed a civilization is the more difficult creativity turns out to be.

Our youngsters remind me of a small child playing with his building blocks. He arranges them as systematically as he can to the limits of his mentality and imagination. Upon reaching the boundaries of his creative ability, he then proceeds to bring the structures crashing to the floor. Because of his limitations he is unable to "create" as the structure grows in complexity. Chaos and clutter often rescue him from his dilemma. Once more he is able to give form and bring order to his endeavors.

All institutions face a similar threat. Government and education are threatened most of all. Revolutionaries along with other young people, the latter merely seeking the easy way, are apparently frustrated by the built-in-demands of specialization and organization. Limited motivation and limited imagination, either or both, mean that youth are not equipped to be as creative as they would like to be on the current scene. They have not been able to resist the temptation to tear down the structures as a result. If they are going to be at all creative, there is a danger that such creativity will come to pass at the high price of destroying the order of society and its major institutions.

4. Humanists

As dangerous as the "young destroyers" may be, institutions probably have more to fear from the new breed of humanists. The reasons for that fear are fairly clear. Humanism cannot tolerate any force that tends to dehumanize people. Today's institutions have acquired considerable notoriety for doing that very thing. In this respect, no institution is absolved of responsibility. Humanists are thereby inclined to be hostile to almost every existing social organization.

According to Roger Shinn's definition:

> Humanism is the appreciation of man and of the values, real and potential, in human life. It esteems man—not as an animal, a machine, or an angel, but as man. It is concerned with the agonies and triumphs of the human spirit, not in any racial or religious or intellectual elite, but in the whole range of history and experience. It may be humble or haughty, accurate or mistaken in its judgments, but always it cherishes humanity.[1]

We have already seen that every institution tends to cherish itself. When human purposes seem to be at odds with those of the institution, the institution refuses to yield to the desires of the people. Its energies are directed to the end of perpetuating itself. Institutions do not always cherish man. They judge him and try to make him conform to their organizational patterns and aims. I know of no institution which puts an individual above itself.

Humanists can hardly accept this reality as far as institutions are concerned. They thrive when humanity seems to be playing second fiddle to other forces in the environment. Humanism grows like a weed when man is not the chief priority on the value scale of culture. Most of all, when people appear to be falling under the controlling influence of institutions, humanism comes rushing to the rescue. It arms for battle against the doomsday threats of depersonalization or dehumanization.

Shinn would not concur with this estimate of modern humanism. He believes that new humanism or "open humanism sees man in his wider setting. It recognizes his kinship with nature, and it acclaims values that have no utilitarian advantage for man." [2]

Nothing would be more pleasant than to be able to agree with Shinn. Perhaps his view is partially accurate. But I cannot believe that it can possibly apply to the relationship between humanism and institutions. Humanism is philosophically hard pressed to acclaim anything that fails to cherish man above itself. Under humanism's aegis man looks so good to himself as to need the warning: "One must stop eating oneself when one tastes best." No matter how much we may want to mollify its stance, humanism cherishes man to the point of absolutizing him. This means that all things are to be subjected to man. The nature of institutions will not allow humanists to play that game.

THE BLIGHT OF NARCISSISM

Humanism cannot achieve the openness which Shinn proposes or describes. It cannot escape the flaw of inevitable narcissism. Such a flaw makes it attractive on the surface. Narcissism provides humanism with a convincing and winsome appeal. In the final analysis, however, narcissistic humanism is a deadly menace.

I realize that I am bucking the current of popular opinion. For that matter, so is the book as a whole. Some extremely competent persons believe that the recovery of humanism represents the best hope for modern man. These advocates are somewhat aware of the dangers of narcissism without recognizing its affinity for humanism. Erich Fromm has gone so far as to argue that humanism aims at getting rid of man's narcissistic malady. He finds support in observing that "all the great humanist religions can be summarized in one sentence: *It is the goal of man to overcome one's narcissism.*" [3]

This may be the goal of great religions, but they will not succeed if they accent their humanistic elements in the process. Narcissism is humanism's ploy. It is embedded in the fiber of the philosophy which purports to overthrow it. Fromm's proposed method for overcoming individual narcissism reveals as much. He comes very close to contending that what is destructive for a single individual can be good for the whole human race. For he suggests that the way to "overcome one's narcissism" is to universalize it. If mankind is enabled to love itself instead of an individual's loving himself, all will be well. Fromm hails that prospect with emotional anticipation: "Not the national holiday, but the 'day of man' would become the highest holiday of the year." [4]

To go along with Fromm increases the chances for stumbling into a quagmire of oversimplification. One might as well prescribe contaminating an entire family with a virus which has attacked one member as the best remedy for the individual who is ill. It seems to me that a quarantine would make far better sense. If narcissism is individually destructive, its universalization would make it universally destructive.

Such a misconstruction can be maintained, however, as long as we depend on nothing more than a clinical interpretation of narcissism. As a clinician, Fromm holds to a simple equation between narcissism and self-love. It is possible, in the light of that meager definition, to suggest that the remedy for self-love is to love all the rest of humanity in its place.

The myth of Narcissus offers a much wider range of possibilities. When I suggest that humanism cannot avoid the blight of narcissism, I am referring to the mythic ideology rather than to what is suggested by the clinical view. Narcissus fell in love with his own image in a reflecting pool. He did not realize that he had been seduced by his own image. He earnestly believed that he was enraptured with the physical beauty of another.

Marshall McLuhan's contemporary interpretation of the myth serves us well at this juncture. He initially reminds us that "Narcissus" comes from the Greek word "narcosis," meaning numbness. He observes that Narcissus was so drugged by unconscious self-love that he could not even respond to Echo. Although she tempted the youth with fragments of his own speech, he did not respond because he could not. Although he was in love with himself and could have been expected to feed devotedly upon his own voice, that self-love was so firmly entrenched in the unconscious as to defy any possibility of becoming overtly apparent.

McLuhan concludes: ". . . the point of this myth is the fact that men at once become fascinated by any extension of themselves in any material other than themselves." [5] If this represents the narcissism of the individual, then humanism is narcissism universalized.

Here then is humanism's insidious threat to every institution. When humanist forces succeed in overcoming individual narcissism by universalizing it, humanity will be infected as a whole. In that case, humankind will love itself while believing that it is open and inclusive enough to love the rest of creation. That menacing process has already gone very far. Even now mankind does not know how to love non-human entities because, no matter what the apparent objects of its love, it is capable only of loving itself.

THINGS AS HUMANIZING AGENTS

Man's relationship to things is good evidence of the previous charge. Man is becoming increasingly convinced that his love of things has contributed to his depersonalization.

I am convinced that he has never loved things as he should. He has loved them only as extensions of himself. When he has felt the pain of depersonalization, the love for self has prompted him to turn on things with blind fury.

Rather than being agents of dehumanization, things are humanizing and personalizing assets. The making of things, as a first example, appears to be a human characteristic. Animals have a very small capacity for manufacturing things or using tools. Exceptions only prove the rule in this regard. On the other hand, it is conceded that human beings have become the makers and users of things because they do not naturally adapt to their environment. However, it would be a mistake to assume that this means that things are merely a necessity that is latent in our humanity. Necessity is not the only "mother of invention." Scientists no longer believe that the beginnings of agriculture originated with men under the burden of necessity. The more that primitive man was hard pressed to find his daily bread, because he was not close to adequate food supplies, the more he had to forage night and day in order to eke out an existence. He had neither the time nor the energy to invent and develop tools with which to conquer the land. His contemporaries, with the good fortune to live near adequate supplies of food, were a different matter. Relieved of the necessity of a hand-to-mouth existence, they were able to give more time and thought to the making of tools. It is likely that they were our first systematic farmers.

The possession of things is also a boon to our humanity. If one wants to humanize the depressed masses in a blighted ghetto, he had better take some good things along with him when he goes on his errands of mercy. Those impoverished people are in need of things. No amount of spiritual blessings and intangible tinkerings can substitute for their need of material and tangible aids. This applies to more than the mere necessities of life. Nothing is more provoking than the carping of affluent "do-gooders" when they are upset because the poor manage to sneak in a few luxuries. A television antenna on a country shack or a slum dwelling in the ghetto is a lovely sight to see. To anyone's insistence that these people need shoes more than television, the retort that television opens up a world too vast to reach by walking is a very good word. For the sake of their humanity they need both shoes and television.

The real issue may now turn the corner. Man is not depersonalized by the love of things. He does not really love things at all. He would be a far better human specimen if he did. We love ourselves as we hasten to acquire things for ourselves. We thirst for the satiated feeling that we have arrived and have kept abreast of our peers. We appear to love things in maintaining that pace.

We really do not love things as things. If we are such hopeless materialists, why is America so rapidly becoming a junk heap of discarded things? What lies behind the cities' problems in finding enough space for land fills? Why do we put up with built-in obsolescence? Why do we trade cars every year or so? Why do we shed good and comfortable clothing for the newest style? Why do we allow lovely old homes to become disheveled shambles? Why do we forget the campus of our alma mater? Why do we walk away from churches with never a backward look? As long as grand old buildings of once thriving enterprise now look out upon a bewildering devastation through the broken spectacles of their shattered panes, no one can convince me that man loves things too much for his own good.

One of the earliest and most ominous signs of personality deterioration and antisocial attitudes is vandalism. A child's consistently wanton destruction of his toys is a clear and early danger signal. If the practice persists, his parents will usually seek professional treatment for their child. That he will continue to destroy things is not their great fear. They are afraid that this behavior means that he may eventually destroy his fellowmen. There must be some logical and unavoidable connection between the gigantic waste of war material and the fact that the entire military complex is taught to hate the enemy. I cannot forget the spectacle of a hate-ridden adolescent, vilifying her parents to their faces in their attractive den, while she flicked her cigarette ashes on the carpet and then stubbed out the cigarette flame on the coffee table. Of course two or more ash trays were within easy reach.

The point is more apparent, to be sure, with the reminder that the very *human* people of Venice are engaged in Herculean efforts to preserve the city and its art treasures. Nor can we easily ignore the implication of an organization which prevents cruelty and exploitation of animals being called the Humane Society. Go a step farther: a girl's love for her clothes makes her no less human. Even the boy, incessantly waxing his car, may see his reflected humanity in its sheen.

TURNING THINGS INTO PERSONS

It would be foolish to argue that there is no connection between things and the process of dehumanization. There is a connection but it does not rest on man's love of things. Furthermore, we are mistaken in the widespread belief that depersonalization is the consequence of persons being turned into things. In other words, we are not so much in danger of being turned into things as we are in danger of turning things into persons. Idolatry makes things into gods. Its modern-day secular counterpart turns things into persons.

In this context, narcissistic humanism and idolatry come very close to being the same evil. Man's fascination with the extensions of himself in nonhuman materials ultimately personalizes those materials. By personalizing the nonpersonal, man's narcissism is better facilitated. He is freer to love that which is more like him, although all the while he is only loving himself.

It is not at all unusual for us to make persons out of our pets. I remember an old lady walking the boardwalk at Atlantic City. She was pushing one of the most elaborate baby carriages I have ever seen. In it were two small dogs dressed in infant finery from baby caps to baby shoes. She was playing the role of a devoted mother.

Many of those who stopped to watch this scene remarked that it was a cute and quaint picture. As for me, I was glad to be rescued from my embarrassment by a small boy. Breaking loose from his mother, he ran to the carriage and knocked the caps off the heads of the dogs. His raucous hoots shattered the air with the demanding sounds of reality.

Turning dogs into persons is neither cute nor quaint. It is unseemly and gross. Turning things into persons is even more so. If we tend to do so with dogs, chances are that we will do the same with things.

The practice may be relatively harmless if it never gets beyond treating dogs like babies or automobiles like mistresses. It seldom stops with that. The next step is the transfer of human responsibility to nonhuman forces. This is the ultimate disaster which narcissistic humanism seems to foster.

Advanced technology is a contributing factor to this undesirable result. We are prone to saddle more complex things with a greater burden of personalized responsibility. If I hit my thumb instead of the nail while using a simple hammer, I know that I am responsible. I may use some generous expletives on the hammer, but I know where the responsibility lies. If the hammer is electronically controlled, the outcome is quite different. I am much more likely to blame the faulty mechanism.

A similar principle applies to modern warfare. If a soldier turns his gun loose on helpless captives in a remote village of Vietnam, he is judged to be guilty of murder in the first degree. If a button energizes a missile or ejects a bomb, killing many more times the number of people killed by the individual soldier, the responsibility of the button pusher is vague and obscure. Technology is deemed to be the culprit.

Technology and narcissistic humanism form a terrible combination. Society may not be able to stand both of them together. Man begins by believing in his love for things which prove to destroy others and himself. He personalizes them to the degree of conferring responsibility upon them. This allows his love to turn to hate when he is faced with his own responsibility. In order to protect himself, he finally blames things for bringing in destruction.

TURNING INSTITUTIONS INTO PERSONS

Institutions are the easiest of all things to turn into persons. It naturally follows that they also lend themselves with great facility to the transfer of responsibility from persons to them. Relationships with institutions are less problematic than a person's connection with other things. Almost every other thing must be made, bought, received as a gift, or stolen by the one who ultimately possesses it. On the other hand, he is born into the family and the nation. He is born again into the church. He is legally required to attend public school. He must somehow relate to business if he is to win his bread.

Man's inevitable relationship with social organizations causes him all the more readily to see them as extensions of himself. By virtue of his narcissistic humanism he even believes that he loves them. That love and his natural dependence upon institutions prompts him to hold them responsible for his well-being. Nothing more is needed to assure his depersonalization. It has occurred with the transfer of responsibility.

Given these circumstances, hostility between humanists and institutions is well nigh unavoidable. At first glance, the latter seem to lend themselves to the ends of narcissistic humanism: the love of oneself in something else which is finally to be held accountable. Despite their apparent acquiescence to this process, institutions never really permit themselves to shoulder such transferred responsibility. They are designed so as to tell persons what to do and to think for them, but they will not be responsible for them. In fact, a person could never retain any kind of individuality within an institution if the latter did become responsible for him. The only kind of individuality that is possible in relationship to institutions is that of a responsible nature. Autonomous individualism is soon forfeited by the person who relates to any kind of institution. Therefore, when a person seeks to transfer his responsibility to an institution, he gives up his individuality and his personhood and is judged to be responsible for having done so.

As a result, man is terribly confused about his relationship to institutions. Since he often wants to evade responsibility for himself, he courts institutions for the purpose of shifting that responsibility onto them. However, since he also wants desperately to be an individual, he shies away from institutions in order to assure that desire. He misconstrues the nature and practice of institutions on both counts. They will not accept the responsibility that must be his, nor do they rob him of individuality as such. They simply will not tolerate autonomous individuality. As we have already seen, institutions accommodate responsible individuals and no one else.

Although he may not see it as such, modern man's dilemma in this regard may find an example in the writings of Kahlil Gibran. I have pondered the recrudescent popularity of Gibran in recent times. *The Prophet,* presumably one of his masterpieces, keeps popping into the wedding ceremonies of those young couples wishing to get away from traditional ceremonies. Parts of *The Prophet*'s counsel to marriage celebrants reads as follows:

> Love one another, but make not a bond of love . . .
> Fill each other's cup but drink not from one cup.
> Give one another of your bread but eat not from the same loaf.
> Sing and dance together and be joyous, but let each one of you be alone,[6]

I take this to mean that marriage partners must not covenant in the category of love. They should be close but not too close. They may be married but not too much married. At all costs they must maintain their individuality. The integrity of their personhood is not to be violated. Their humanity must be protected against the institution of marriage.

In short, couples are taught to relate in love without having to face their individual responsibility for one another when they are no longer in love. Refusing to shoulder that kind of responsibility, they are free to complain that the marriage was a bad idea in the first place if and when things should go wrong.

In this as well as other instances, institutions are being used as scapegoats for a majority of modern and very human defects. Man is busily hanging his sins on the horns of these "institutional scapegoats." He hopes to push them off a cliff carrying his faults with them in their plunge to death. Little does he realize that most of his humanity will go over the edge at the same time.

5. Unbiblical Churchmen

A specific question now begins to assert itself: Who is the greatest menace to the institution of religion which is called the church? The unbiblical churchman gets my vote.

So far as I know, the young destroyers have not yet bombed a church although they have blasted away at almost everything else. It could be that young people consider the church too insignificant to justify the risk. In any event, they show greater facility for ignoring it than for destroying it.

The same may be said with respect to humanists. Their irrevocable antipathy for institutions is less intense toward the church than to its counterparts. There seems to be a tacit agreement between the church and humanists, even when they are members, as many are. They will not bother the church if it promises to do the same for them.

The unbiblical churchman is far more dangerous to the church than the rest. Since he is closer to the ecclesiastical vital organs, he can strike deadlier blows. This does not mean that he is a subversive, deliberately plotting the downfall of organized religion. It is his innocence which makes him dangerous. He wants to spiritualize and thereby purify the church. He hopes to rekindle its evangelistic fires. He insists upon salvation in terms of personal experience with Jesus Christ and not enlistment in a church. The unbiblical churchman is usually convinced that these dreams are doomed unless the church is rescued from the pernicious effects of organization. He knows the strength of Peter Berger's position:

> . . . the Christian faith demands a personal decision. No amount of religious "growth" or social involvement in religious groups can release us from this demand. This decision is for Jesus Christ, not for the religious institution.[1]

Before one agrees with Berger, he should raise at least one question. Are Jesus Christ and the church mutually exclusive in his view? It is said that one's decision has to be for Jesus Christ and not for the institution. What is not settled in this approach to the matter is the manner of one's decision for Christ. It is decidedly problematic for anyone to assume that he may make a decision for Christ without reference to the religious institution, i.e., the church. It is decidedly unbiblical for anyone to ignore the scriptural testimony that the church is the body of Christ. And it is decidedly illogical for anyone to think that he may be related to Christ without His body.

Without similarly emphasizing experience with Jesus Christ, the late Paul Tillich insisted upon the sectarian note of personal decision in Protestantism with the same vigor as Berger:

> Each Protestant, each layman, each minister . . . has to decide for himself whether a doctrine is true or not, whether a prophet is a true or a false prophet, whether a power is demonic or divine. Even the Bible cannot liberate him from this responsibility, for the Bible is a subject of interpretation. . . . For the Protestant, individual decision is inescapable.[2]

In these respective positions both Berger and Tillich serve to quicken my sectarian and Baptist blood. Individual or personal decision for Jesus Christ has been the manifest of my denominational forebears and I have gladly embraced that legacy. But Tillich's premise is no more immune to question than is Berger's. Is it sufficient to say that "the Bible is *a* subject of interpretation?" A more accurate position is that "the Bible is *the* subject of interpretation" in a unique and precise way. That would be to contend that one's individual interpretation of Scripture cannot be a unilateral and isolated decision. The authority of the Bible is not simply at the mercy of its interpreter. Nor can we arrive at conclusions, parallel to those of Scripture, without resorting to Scripture.

> Whoever, without justification, continues to talk about God in avoidance of the Word of God, talks God to death. And whoever, avoiding the Word of God, forgoes talk about God, silences God to death. In order that God be neither talked to death nor silenced to death, the Word of God demands undivided . . . attention.[2]

Thus has Eberhard Jüngel argued that although the Bible may be "*a* subject of interpretation," it is the Word, which can neither be displaced nor dismissed because it is *the* subject of that interpretation.

To speak of God or Christ, while avoiding the Word of God, is to sign their obituary as far as the speaker is concerned. That seems to be the present inclination of the unbiblical churchman. The irony is supreme. In his attempt to magnify God and Christ by deciding for them and not for the institution, he actually subverts his own purpose by means of scriptural excision.

Perhaps the unbiblical churchman intuitively realizes that he cannot get rid of the religious institution without circumventing the authority of the Scriptures. His highly spiritualized version necessitates the scrapping of tangibles: both Bible and church. The interplay between church, Bible, and personal religion has made for a dilemma-ridden history of Christianity. The apostolic church wrote and compiled the Scriptures. Subsequently, it was the Roman Catholic church which decided the canon. This led to an early assumption that it was the power and prerogative of the Roman Catholic church to decide and determine the meaning of Scripture.

Not until the time of Martin Luther was the Roman Catholic stranglehold on the Scriptures broken. His aggressive doctrine of the "priesthood of believers" found a powerful and willing ally in the invention of the printing press.

The Bible was then widely disseminated among the people and progressively replaced the Roman Catholic church as the highest authority for faith and conduct. Rigid biblical literalism was the inevitable outcome. Bibliolatry and the Reformation went hand in hand.

The sectarian movements, beginning in the sixteenth century, delivered the earliest jolts to literalism. "Soul competency" became a synonym for the doctrine of the priesthood of believers. The individual no longer needed any human intermediary between God and himself. His interpretation of Scripture would suffice. Personal experience with Jesus Christ constituted the highest authority of all. That represented the core of sectarian religion.

Some groups carried this idea farther than some others. For example, Horton Davies has drawn an interesting comparison between Baptists and Quakers as to the degree of the doctrine's entrenchment within the "free churches."

> Though Baptist ministers did not ordinarily preach from a Sermon manuscript, theirs was a serious attempt to expound the Scriptures, their primary authority. Their extemporary preaching was an attempt to allow the Word of God to be driven home to the people by the illuminating and confirming Spirit. . . . as a liturgical criterion Scripture was primary for the Baptists and secondary for the Quakers; the Holy Spirit was secondary for the Baptists and primary for the Quakers.[4]

It is something more than coincidence that Quakers or Friends, to this day, are less institutional than most religious bodies. Although there are other contributing factors, not the least of these is the secondary consideration that is accorded the Scriptures. Other highly sectarian churches are of similar ilk. Furthermore, the fact that Baptists give great attention to the place of the Spirit in their lives partially explains their own comparatively loose-knit organization.

Time and space do not permit an exhaustive treatment of the confusion between Holy Spirit and "inner spirit" that is so characteristic of most of these communions in question. The Holy Spirit and the church are not antithetical. It is the people of the "inner spirit" who have most difficulty with the church. At this juncture, I am equating "inner spirit" with the human rather than the Holy Spirit.

UNBIBLICAL YOUTH

Among the world's youth, unbiblical types have established or joined the "Jesus cult." The majority of them are disillusioned with contemporary cultural values and are disenchanted with the church. They have dropped out of most forms of the establishment and have dropped in on Jesus.

"Jesus Freaks" have their counterparts in square society. Less conspicuous but probably more powerful are Campus Crusade for Christ, Inter-Varsity Fellowship, Young Life, Youth for Christ, and the fast-growing Fellowship of Christian Athletes. These are well-financed and adequately staffed organizations of middle-class high school and college students. It is not uncommon for them to combine testimonies with expensive trips to beach or ski resorts. For the most part, these young squares are still in the churches. At the same time, there can be no question as to their primary loyalty. It rests with the "Jesus cult" syndrome.

Personal experience, spiritual power, biblical illiteracy or literalism — both sides of the same coin — are their trademarks. They are short on "God language." "Jesus talk" is very big. They cannot as yet be moved by criticism even as strong as that of Jüngel. Speaking of personal experience with Jesus Christ, he argues:

> ... even this experience, according to the witness of the New Testament, is certainly not to be had without God. One cannot experience how one relates to Jesus Christ without experiencing how one relates to God. For God alone made Jesus to be the one he is; Jesus did not cause himself to be who he is. ...[5]

Such cautions notwithstanding, our youngsters proceed with their witness to Jesus. An earnest co-ed, miniskirted, blond, and beautiful, told us how Jesus helped her with her examination at college. "You wouldn't believe how much He helped me," she almost cooed. "In fact, He helped me so much that I debated about signing the honor pledge that I had neither given nor received help on my test."

The outcome is always inevitable. An unbiblical courtship with Jesus is one of dismemberment or disembodiment. That is, He is pulled away from His Body, which is the church.

In an aside, these young enthusiasts deserve more admiration than criticism. They point up the superficiality of their counterparts, young activists proposing to bring in the kingdom by their own sweat and by their own calendar. They also "have the number" of suave liberals who worship at the altar of relativity. And their trumpets give a clearer note than the uncertain sound of "new morality" and "situation ethics."

If the church can enlist the members of the Jesus cult in the foreseeable future, the church may expect brighter days. It needs some of their piety. The evangelistic zeal is sorely lacking in the religious establishment. Their unembarrassed witness is refreshing in these days of sophisticated tolerance of any or all beliefs. Their militance may bring a healing shame to the timid Christian.

UNBIBLICAL ADULTS

Were it not for unbiblical adults in the church, this happy prospect of youth putting some of this evangelistic zeal back into the church would augur greater possibility for fulfillment. Instead of trying to institutionalize the faith of the youngsters, they try to mimic their worst characteristics.

Most adults would not identify openly with the more bizarre types of the Jesus cult. In their own way, however, they manage to put their churches in the worst possible light. They try to be very spiritual. They are the kind who clamor about putting "Christ back into Christmas" each time the season arrives. As a rule they buy and sell, give and receive, and go head over heels in debt like everyone else at Christmas, but they always manage to be cleansed from their sins by washing themselves in the "Tide" of guilt. This is a form of religious pollution.

This aversion to all that is not spiritual means trouble

for the religious organization. It is unpopular because it is tangible and visible.

As I have already mentioned but briefly, today's spiritual people confuse spiritual feelings with the visitation of the Holy Spirit. They are ignorant of the connection between the church and the Holy Spirit. The fact that the classic setting for the Spirit's coming is at baptism does not mean that the Spirit is bound exclusively to the body or its sacraments, but there can be no doubt that baptism is a rite of the church. In that rite, the convert is not characterized as possessed of a spiritual feeling arising from the stuff of his own emotions. He is filled with the Spirit, which is not naturally his own but is given to him by the power and the will of God.

A NECESSARY EVIL

"Spiritual people" usually concede that the church is a necessary evil. Therefore they continue to support the necessities of church. They will serve in administrative tasks. Quite often they are willing teachers in the church school. Quite happily, they assume as much financial responsibility as do those who recognize and affirm the value of organized religion.

In a sense they suffer the same kind of frustration which plagued Martin Luther throughout the span of his reform. For the purpose of that reform, Luther found it absolutely necessary to attack the institutions and structures of Roman Catholicism.

His goals were inextricably linked with their abolition. He failed to see the importance of other forms and institutions for the Reformed Church. Little heed was given to this problem. As a result, Luther was never quite prepared to

> ... come to terms with the necessity either of renewing the given structures or of creating new structures, which would, of course, inevitably be in need of eventual renewal. No trial oppressed Luther's spirit more often in his later years than this recognition that structure was inevitable, combined as the recognition was with a candid awareness that the institutions

now being erected were not necessarily superior to those which had (often against Luther's advice) been swept away.[6]

As was true with Luther, most churchmen are presently aware of the necessity for organized religion. It is something they cannot do without no matter how much they would prefer to be able to do so. Unfortunately, there seems to be a streak in human nature which prompts us to meet necessity with apathy. This is a curious tendency. It would appear more logical if we gave more attention to what is necessary than to what is optional. Since a matter is necessary, we should make the very best of that necessity.

Government is necessary. When the people respond apathetically, it becomes tyrannical and bureaucratic. When business is met with apathy, it settles into nondescript sterility. When the church is met with apathy, it becomes dull and graceless.

Necessity produces apathy. Optionals elicit imagination, ingenuity, industriousness, and enthusiasm. Our values and practices are certainly strangely askew.

To make matters worse, Rollo May advises that hate is not the opposite of love. Apathy is. That is the sad commentary of what has happened to the church at the hands of its own people. It would have more hope if they hated it.

6. The Idolatrous Risk

The more one emphasizes the institutional character of the church, as I have been doing, the more he becomes suspect as a practitioner in idolatry. Organized religion inevitably smacks of an effort to domesticate God and to confine him to worldly structures. There have always been strong countermeasures against that and every other form of idolatry in the whole gamut of Judeo-Christian religion.

The great outcry against idolatry by the Jews is quite understandable. They conceived their exile and even possibly their Egyptian bondage to have been the direct results of idolatrous worship and practices. It is not at all surprising that the stinging satire of Isaiah 44 should appear when and where it did. Its polemic against idolatry fitted with the bitter mood of the exiles.

Little can be said in defense of idolatry as such. It is the ultimate misrepresentation of God. He becomes what man makes of Him and is thus the object of human manipulation. No heresy exceeds that of idolatry.

At the same time, none of the great western religions have been able to escape running the risk of idolatry. This is particularly the case with Judaism and Christianity. Their history is replete with episodes of the idolatrous risk. Outstanding among these occurrences were the institutionalizations of Yahweh in the ark of the covenant, in the Jerusalem temple, and in the synagogues. Each of these external structures represented a dwelling place of God. As a consequence the ark was untouchable. The temple's inner sanctuary was holy ground not to be violated by human intrusion. Although the synagogue was not enhanced to this degree, it was nevertheless in the same category as the ark and the temple.

Cautions against idolizing the ark and the temple are prominently recorded in the Scriptures. Uzzah's death as a result of touching the ark convinced David that God had some reservations about being carted to Jerusalem in a box. Three months elapsed before David dared to escort the ark on to Jerusalem.

Second Samuel includes Nathan's enjoinder against David's building a temple as the house of God. The Lord reputedly tells Nathan to remind David, "I have not dwelt in a house since the day I brought up the people of Israel from Egypt to this day, but I have been moving about in a tent for my dwelling" (2 Samuel 7:6). This writer apparently ignores 1 Samuel 3:3f., which tells us that the prophet was called by the Lord when "Samuel was lying down within the temple of the Lord, where the ark of God was." It seems clear then that there was a temple at Shiloh. Then, too, Solomon later on reports that David did not build the temple because he had been too busy fighting the enemies of Israel. So these cautions against the institutionalization of God are not unmixed.

Of more importance is the understanding of God in the combined Judeo-Christian theology. As opposed to a remote and distant deity, too holy even to touch a fallen world, He is One who acts in history. "God was in Christ reconciling the world . . ." (2 Corinthians 5:19). Our theology cannot avoid anthropomorphic descriptions of God. Furthermore, it is the nature of man to mark the time and place of the significant events in his life. The first kiss between lovers, the birthplace of a famous person, the first tree from which we fell, and the scene of one's baptism come to be significant places in our memories. In like manner, Jacob built a monument at Bethel because of his meeting with the Lord on that spot. Such are the materials of the idolatrous risk.

Salvation history would have been much poorer if our forebears had refused to run that risk. The ark of the covenant bordered on idolatry; but ponder the consequence had those homeless Jews been without a symbol of Yahweh's presence as they walked the tortuous trail to the Promised Land. The synagogue implied a form of domesticating God. Could his people have kept faith without this symbol that God could be in distant lands far from their home? Would the Jew have struggled back to Jerusalem out of exile had he not been determined to rebuild the Jerusalem temple?

It stands to reason that the intense and plentiful injunctions against idolatry in Judeo-Christian Scriptures are there because the faith is vulnerable to idolatry. This is a risk to overcome rather than to avoid. The Christian must take that chance, coming through the ordeal with faith in God rather than in his representations.

INSTITUTIONS AND LIFE'S MEANING

Idolatry is made possible by the materialization of a spiritual reality. When Jacob enshrined his meeting with God in stone at Bethel, he encouraged the possibility of sacralizing the pillar in the place of the spiritual event. This is the ever-present danger prompted by the religious institution. Nothing else ever skirts closer to idolatry.

This strongly tempts all of us to strive for a faith which will not be corrupted by the church. It seems quite apparent that unorganized religion is less susceptible to this particular form of corruption. However attractive this approach may be, it will create a far greater problem than that of idolatry. It propels us toward meaninglessness. As a matter of fact, persons cannot have meaningful lives unless they participate in institutions.

This dogmatic assertion needs the support of persuasive argument if it is to stand. Rollo May is my first witness. He has written:

> ... that every *meaning has within it a commitment*. ... Meaning has no meaning apart from intention. ...
> Cognition, or knowing, and cognation, or willing, then go together. We could not have one without the other.[1]

I contend that these three—intention, commitment, and meaning — are best brought together by an institution. Intention, for example, is commitment in embryonic form. Before we are committed to anything, we must first intend it. Furthermore, that intention falls short of commitment until it takes on the form and substance of institution. Jacob had his dream and made his vow. That vow was not substantiated until he institutionalized his vow or intention by erecting a monument. This made his intention visible to others and prevented his backing away from his vow without embarrassment and public ridicule. Such institutionalizing, in turn, fulfills the overriding demand for meaning. Institutions more effectively socialize our commitments and thereby give them meaning for us as well as others.

Peter Berger is my second witness.

> To deny reality as it has been socially defined is to risk falling into irreality, because it is well-nigh impossible in the long run to keep up alone and without social support one's own counterdefinitions of the world. ... The ultimate danger of such separation, however, is the danger of meaninglessness. This danger is the nightmare *par excellence,* in which the individual is submerged in a world of disorder, senselessness and madness.[2]

Man's intention and commitment achieve their necessary meaning when they take place within an organization for the promotion of a cause, which is the definition of an institution. Intention and commitment, when they are not brought to public view by an institution, will almost invariably, along with the individual, become "submerged in a world of disorder, senselessness and madness."

It seems apparent that we live in a day of uncommitted people. The majority seems to lack intention and thus to suffer from a loss of meaning. As one searches out the reasons for this malaise, one central factor stands out. There is a relationship of cause and effect between anti-institutional people and uncommitted ones. These are reciprocal postures: first one playing upon the other and in turn being influenced by the other.

The popular jargon of anti-institutional youth is illustrative. Theirs is also the jargon of the uncommitted. "Involvement" has replaced words such as "commitment" or "dedication." Involvement means to be swept up from the periphery into the center of things and there to become inextricably entangled. One may become involved without intending to do so. He simply waits for some force to engulf him.

Equally indicative is the concept of being "turned on" or "turned off." Either phrase is empty of intention and commitment. It is consequently devoid of meaning. One who waits to be "turned on" or "turned off," as the case may be, places responsibility on another rather than himself. In the first instance, individuals often blame teachers or preachers for failing to "turn them on." They make no efforts of their own to be instructed or incited. By the same token, if they lose their interest in a subject or their passion for a cause, the blame rests with whatever person has "turned them off." Instead of being highly spirited people, as they think themselves to be, they are more like light switches being flipped up and down at the will of others.

The desire for "happenings" comes from the same lack of commitment. "Happenings" demand no planning or commitment. If a "happening" takes place, all is well. If it does not, nothing is lost because nothing had been expected.

These are passive words without exception. They convey a wish to be acted upon rather than to act. In a sense they are the essence of passive irresponsibility. It is small wonder that this is an age of anti-establishment mentality. Institutions are not geared to "involve" passively uncommitted people. They ferret out people who possess intentionality.

Then they insist that these intentions take on the stability and force of tangible and visible forms.

ANOTHER RISK — HYPOCRISY

This brings us to consider another risk which is most certainly a first cousin to idolatry. Hypocrisy is its name. As idolatry is a distortion of worship, hypocrisy is a distortion of commitment.

Worried at its decline in morality and the breakdown of its integrity, this generation has become especially sensitive to the sins of hypocrisy. Man is taking every precaution to ward off the fact or even the appearance of hypocrisy. Next to absolute purity, his best safeguard is to divest himself of every intention and possible commitment. If one takes no position and gives no notice of his values and beliefs, he gives no reason for others to call him a hypocrite. With nothing to live up to, there is nothing to be let down. Before one can pretend, he must intend.

Institutions apparently demand the hypocritical risk for the same reasons that they demand the idolatrous risk. If and when a person joins a church, for example, he immediately sets himself up as a possible hypocrite. Faith has been declared. All people are his brothers in Christ. He must love God and neighbor. The redemptive mission has been joined. The will of God is his mandate.

I know of no person who has ever lived up to these intentions. To whatever degree his failure, the person is a hypocrite in like degree. This is the chance which men must take. A society of men committed to no worthwhile values and without noble intentions is a meaningless and dreadful society. More than a few critics have blasted the church in my presence because "it is full of hypocrites." They have been fairly well shocked by my reply, "You are so right. Thank God."

INSTITUTIONS AND SOCIETY

I have been confessing the possible inclination of institutions to idolatry and hypocrisy. I have argued that these are probable and necessary risks if man is to have faith and life is to have meaning. It is a relief not to have to confess in answering another criticism of institutions. Large numbers of people are convinced that institutions are a drag upon free, joyful, and wholesome relationships between persons. Since society itself is largely a matter of personal relationships, institutions now stand accused of being detrimental to society in general.

Such accusative criticisms have more current fashion than real substance. The truth is that institutions are creative instruments for the making of society or culture. They are also a boon to good personal relationships. "The fundamental dialectic process of society," in Berger's view, "consists of three moments, or steps. These are externalization, objectivation, and internalization." [3]

Externalization is the consistent pouring of one's humanity into his environment. All society or culture initially depends upon this kind of action. It takes place as persons participate in their wider communities.

Objectivation occurs when what has been externalized tends to become a thing in itself. We have already seen how this takes place so far as institutions are concerned. Having become a thing in itself, that which man has projected now begins to shape him even to the point of some control. The English language provides an example. It was humanly produced rather than arising spontaneously from natural sources. Soon, however, its producers became its captives. It became their primary means of communication with others of their kind. Those of us born subsequently into that same culture have been bound to the same kind of communication. Automobiles, airplanes, plumbing, banking, credit cards, and garbage collection fall into the same category. Although human beings brought them into existence, they now determine the life-style of their originators.

Internalization is the third step. It occurs when what has been externalized and objectivated is inwardly appropriated by individuals or groups. Although these three steps are virtually simultaneous, the order in which they are mentioned has significant implications. The general assumption that values begin with the individual and are then shared with society is unmerited. As Berger has observed (cf. p. 59), one cannot deny reality as it is socially defined without falling into irreality. An individual's sense of value can hardly be authenticated until it becomes a part of the social process. After this has occurred, he may appropriate its priorities with assurance. In short, man gives no more values to culture than he takes from it. His individual values come as much from the outside in as they go from the inside out.

Nothing is better designed and equipped for the process of externalization, objectivation, and internalization than is the institution. Let us now turn to a look at these three steps as they characterize social relationships between persons.

Institutions serve as the major channels through which individuals project in the environment. In other words, they are the main paths of our externalization. Their instrumentality in this respect has never been greater than in the highly mobile society of the present. People tend to become rootless in the perpetual motion they must endure by virtue of economic and social ambition as well as business necessities. When they arrive in a new place, they join with the environment through the existing institutions. They cluster in schools, clubs, shopping centers, neighborhood groups, and churches. Without institutions, persons would be hard put ever to touch ground in their new surroundings.

Institutional objectivation enhances personal relationships in three important ways. First of all, institutions are a primary means for sustaining personal relationships once they are begun. A going business enterprise has kept many disaffected partners together long enough for them to effect eventual reconciliation. Social and civic clubs serve similar purposes. This is exceptionally characteristic of churches. A younger minister once came to me for advice. His church was breaking apart. Conservatives and liberals were at loggerheads. The generation gap was exacting a severe toll. I suggested that he concentrate on winning loyalty and love for the church from both sides. This sounded much too tactical and impersonal for my idealistic colleague. He was incensed to the point of accusing me in that vein. He may have been right in his impressions of me, but I had answered him with utter seriousness. Love for the institution by both sides seemed to be the only solution to his problem.

In the second place, the objectivity of institutions conditions people to take one another for granted. There is much more good than bad in this practice. Members of a community of faith may justifiably assume mutual and reciprocal loyalty, friendship, and dependability. Goodwill is taken for granted. Without elemental assumptions of this kind, relationships have to be tested and perennially reinforced. Friendships must often be affirmed and renewed at very picayune levels. They demand so much attention that the genuine values of relationship are often obscured. Congregational fusses provide cynics with ammunition for a contrary argument. The larger view, however, will convince most of us that the cynic is usually beating the air at this point.

Objectivation by institutions, as a third instance, orders our relationships in healthy ways. This relieves us of having to contrive times and places for their cultivation.

I was once a member of a golf foursome which grew to be a marvelous institution! In addition to me it was made up of a Methodist wholesale grocer, a lawyer who was vice-president of his synagogue, and an atheistic manager of an apartment complex. The lawyer and I were always matched against the other two. Every Saturday (the Jew was outvoted by the Gentiles) we joined each other on the first tee at 12:21 P.M. No communication was necessary unless one of us could not play for "providential reasons." In that event, the "dropout" called the grocer, who was chairman of arrangements. We elected the atheist for our scorekeeper.

Since he did not believe in God, he did not believe in grace. This made him the most honest man in the group. The rest of us might have tested divine mercy in the heat of a close match.

This kind of order is a boon to good and lasting relationships. People relax in their awareness that they will see one another at work, at school, or in church. Certainty of contact with one another is a basis for friendship. It also burdens each person with the responsibility for making sure that he conducts himself as a friend rather than as a hostile.

Institutions offer persons the best chance for the movement of internalization. Not only do they develop personal exchanges, they gather people around causes. Good relationships are comprised of "shoulder-to-shoulder" or "side-by-side" as well as "face-to-face" postures. As persons join in common causes, they inevitably appropriate for themselves those values which are reflected in their common mission. This is the essence of internalization. The mission of the church may become the pilgrimage of the person. Two people on the same pilgrimage must come together, or one or the other has to take a detour. Good personal relationships are significantly influenced by the fact of mutual mission.

IN CHRIST

Even if none of the foregoing arguments can be substantially authenticated, the institution of religion is a scriptural mandate. The biblical witness cannot be ignored or denied in this respect. The church as an institution gives no quarter to the private person. It knows nothing of humanism's lover of mankind. It severely judges the unbiblical pietist wanting to carry Jesus in his heart. As far as the revolutionary is concerned, although the Scriptures speak his language to some extent, their affirmation of the religious institution circumscribes his freedom for irresponsible and violent action.

Be reminded that the Bible has far more to say about the person being in Christ than about Christ being in the person. William Barclay sees this so clearly in the writings of the apostle Paul:

> Every man who writes or speaks a great deal has favorite phrases. . . . Paul had such a phrase, and the phrase is *in Christ*. . . .
> This phrase is not so much the essence of Paul's theology, as it is the summary of his whole religion. . . . Of all the letters which Paul ever wrote, it is absent in only one—in *2 Thessalonians*.[4]

Martin Dibelius was equally convinced and convincing if not more so. Not only did he agree as to the importance Paul placed on being *in Christ,* he also believed that the apostle used the phrase as a synonym for being in the church. Dibelius made this observation:

> He uses the phrase not only about his life's special experiences; he can say of every Christian that he is "in Christ Jesus", and the words "Adronicus and Junias [who were] in Christ before me" (Romans 16:7) simply indicate an earlier entry into the Church—Paul, in fact, still has no word for "Christian" or "Christianity," and therefore has to use words meaning a person's membership of the "body of Christ" [the Church] or his activity in it.[5]

The importance of being *in Christ* is reflected in the two major sacraments of the church. Baptism and Communion are the practices of almost every Christian body and in that order. Unless and until one is baptized, he is not eligible for Communion. The church insists on this without exception and without apology. The symbolism behind its insistence is significant and revealing.

Depending upon its mode, baptism represents immersion into Christ or the putting on of Christ by sprinkling or pouring. Either style baptizes the candidate so that he is *in Christ* either symbolically or sacramentally or both.

Communion symbolizes taking Christ into oneself. The "body" is eaten. The "blood" is consumed. The concept of Christ being in the person is thereby served. Of genuine importance, however, is that a person must be in Christ before Christ may be in him. Baptism precedes Communion.

Neither of the sacraments is an individual matter. Baptism into Christ is baptism into His body which is the church. Baptism into the church is also baptism by the church. Private baptism in any ecclesiastical body is an inexplicable heresy. As for Communion, Paul enjoined the Corinthians against eating and drinking without taking notice of the faithful community; those who do so "will be guilty of desecrating the body and blood of the Lord" (1 Corinthians 11:27, NEB). *The New English Bible* is more explicit on this theme than are the other major translations. In the tradition established by the King James Version, which specifies the "Lord's body," *The New English Bible* capitalizes the key word: "For he who eats and drinks eats and drinks judgement on himself if he does not discern the Body" (1 Corinthians 11:29, NEB).

Thus it is that the church, in view of the nature and sequence of its major sacraments, challenges the myth of the inner man and his internal religion. One is not a Christian by virtue of what is within him. He is Christian by virtue of his being in the community of faith. I am in agreement with B. F. Skinner:

> . . . the Inner Man is most often invoked when the behavior to be explained is unusual with respect to other parts of a man's behavior, or fragmentary with respect to his behavior as a whole or beyond the control of the rest of him as a person. But the "rest of him" must also be explained, and when all parts have been assembled, the Inner Man behaves very much like the Outer.[6]

And why? It happens this way because as a participant in society man internalizes its values until they become his own. They proceed from the social to the individual level. In that light, if man is to have meaningful inner values he must participate in the social process and join with the institutions which inform and energize it. Religiously speaking, he must be in the institutional church. Since his inner faith conforms to his outer experience, that which externally affects him is of utmost importance. If he tries to go it alone, privately and inwardly, he may miss the inner value he seeks. He could become like what Peter deVries has one of his characters say of another: "Down deep he's shallow."

Skinner pursues his premise with an intriguing question:

Can the Inside Story be written in another way? Instead of looking inside to see what crossed the gap when man was created, why not build a machine that behaves like a man and see what must be put into it to make it work?[7]

Skinner does not admit how very biblical he tends to be. His recommendation is not another or new way of writing the Inside Story. This suggested alternative did not originate with the author of *Walden Two*. The copyright belongs to the author of Genesis 2. Centuries ago he wrote: ". . . then the Lord God formed man of dust from the ground, and breathed into his nostrils the breath of life; and man became a living being" (Genesis 2:7).

If man is once again to come truly alive, let him be in the body of Christ. This will give him the form he must have into which the spirit may come once more.

7. The Sacred and the Profane

Can the institutional church come alive today as did God's dusty man of Genesis? There are those who insist that it cannot as long as it remains an institution. In their view the religious establishment has no room for the Spirit. Either the church wards off the Spirit altogether or drives it out if it manages to get through organized religion's security guard. The institutional church is like that antiseptic human house of Jesus' parable in Matthew 12. It alienates "spirit" of any kind. It cannot replace an unclean spirit with the Holy Spirit. Because the institutional is an empty shell, its future presages a time when it will be demonized many times over — a dreadfully haunted house of demonic anonymity.

For even the most ardent defender of organized religion to shrug off this accusation is the height of foolishness. Too much of the evidence is against him. Institutions have proven their antipathy to the Spirit in countless cases. This poses a profound dilemma for the argument I am trying to wage. How can I defend the concept of institution if institution is an enemy of spirit and the Holy Spirit? If institution is a primary factor in the despiritualization of human existence, is it not also true that its would-be destroyers should be aided in their very commendable endeavors? How can anyone justify his opposition to those who strive to in-spirit humanity once again?

Any answer will have to emerge from a very stubborn paradox. It is true that institutions kill the spirit. It is just as true that homeless and anonymous spirits become unclean and assume the destructive characteristics possessed by every *diamon*. In other words, spirit or *diamon* without a place is an unnamed dread. Since institutions define time and place, they tend to identify spirit and guard against its destructive anonymity.

For example, the Holy Spirit is not anonymous. It is holy as God is holy. The spirit is to be sent by Jesus Christ. It is to come when he goes away and it will come to his people. As a consequence, the institution of faith waits for the coming of the Spirit of Christ.

But does this not construct an impossible situation? If institutions alienate and suppress the Spirit, how can they also serve as its most likely abiding place? This paramount paradox lights up the essentiality of the institutional church. It strongly suggests that the church is the only institution which can possibly receive and be amenable to the Holy Spirit. Other institutions may develop their own spirits: "spirit of 76," team spirit, club spirit, *et al*. Only the church may incorporate a Spirit not its own, holy as God is holy, and sent at the bidding of Jesus Christ.

This surely means that the church cannot simply be another institution. It must be a unique establishment. Perforce it cannot be anything other than a sectarian institution. Although sectarian and institution are thought to be mutually exclusive, such is the combination of the religious organization. While sectarian connotes the coming of the Holy Spirit, institution connotes the home to which Holy Spirit comes.

As a sectarian institution the church will not repeat the sectarian mistake of former years. Franklin Littell has made an observation about the Anabaptists, which may apply to the entire sectarian movement:

> . . . the Anabaptists counted the fallen condition of the Church *from the days of Constantine until the beginning of their own movement. The Reformers also belonged to the period of the Fall.* The Anabaptists said that the revival began with Luther and Zwingli but when the reformers clung to the old idea of Christendom, the radicals counted them out.[1]

This meant that the more vehement sectarians insisted that the church had been actually nonexistent between biblical or apostolic times and the initiation of their own religious venture. That Thomas Muntzer could refer to Martin Luther as "Brother Soft-Life" indicates the contempt with which sectarians viewed the noble work of the reformers. They were sectarians without the stabilizing influence of institution. No institutional people could have possibly contended that there had been no church whatsoever throughout those tumultuous and productive years.

These sectarians, who claimed to recreate the church for their age, were restorers rather than reformers. And they were wrong. To say as much is not to discount the valuable contributions they made. It is to oppose the heresy that the church actually ceased to exist from the days of Constantine until they came along.

Although my theological and ecclesiastical roots have been nurtured in sectarian gardens, I find more compatibility with the confession of Alex Vidler than with a host of sectarians:

> It is the whole Christian movement in history . . . into which I am grateful to have been received, which I want to see continuing, however much it needs to be further developed and enlarged, reformed or refined. . . .
> I believe that men need to belong to a concrete community which is universal in principle, and which holds them together as men (the first and the last Adam) and not merely as citizens or as members of a professional or sectional club; a community which represents and sustains a way of life and a way of thought that are traditional and deeply rooted in the past but also open to change and development as the dynamism of history moves on. . . .[2]

Every self-described endeavor to recreate or restore the church, in this era, is an insult to that "community . . . traditionally and deeply rooted in the past. . . ." The church has been from the time of the resurrection. To think or act contrarily to this reality is a heinous presumption. Every such presumption must be countered with the strongest arguments to the contrary. These arguments are only possible, however, in the light of the fact that the church is an institution. Had it not been, it could not have survived.

No one can deny that the church often became a thing in itself across the centuries. It alienated the Spirit until its vitality was little more than institutional momentum. It lost its moorings from the past and saw the future through almost lifeless eyes. It became little more than a shell of what it was intended to be. Because it has appeared so often as little more than an empty hulking shell of unfulfilled promise, there has been the perennial ambition to abolish it and to start all over again. But the church cannot be treated as if it were no more than an obsolete building or an anachronistic form that is standing around in the way. It has always been the embodiment of God's purpose and the landing strip for the Spirit of the risen Lord.

This is the reason that the church must be a sectarian institution. Sectarian enthusiasm and receptivity to the Spirit are keys to the vitality of the church. It cannot rely on the nurture of this world for its life. Although they are in the world, its people are not of this world. As an institution, the church is very much a part of social history. As a *sectarian* institution, the church finds its life not in worldly resources but in the offerings of the Spirit.

It has always been hard for the church to turn away from the nourishing resources of the world. Linus, the security-blanketed character in "Peanuts," of the comic section, provides one of the chief reasons.

"If I ever get to be a theologian," he announces, "I'm going to be what they call a 'theologian in the marketplace.' "

"So you can reach the people?" Charlie Brown asks.

"No, that's where the lettuce is!"

Despite these kinds of difficulties, the church always comes close to being a superfluous institution when it loses its sectarian sense of being an institution apart from the world. In this respect, Peter Berger cuts with a keen blade.

> One may begin by admiring Christians for their political involvements. But then one must also admire all the others, including the Black Muslims and the atheists, who share these involvements. If the political struggles have become the very reason for being a Christian in the first place, this reason will soon lose plausibility the more one involves oneself in these struggles. If secular aims define the mission of the Church in society, the conclusion that the Church is finally unnecessary is inevitable, no matter how noble the secular aims may be.[3]

Not without considerable hesitancy do I venture to point to a present example of the sectarian institution. Since I am a clergyman within its ranks, it may appear to be a presumption for me to suggest the phenomenon of Southern Baptists. Let the reader be assured that I do not believe that Southern Baptists are models to be copied in all respects. Even in this present reference they leave much to be desired. However, they do represent some ascertainable aspects of sectarian institutions.

Although they insist that they are not a "church" in the sense of the Roman Catholic church, the Anglican church, or the Presbyterian church, no religious body in American life is more institutionalized. Madison Avenue meets its match at the Southern Baptist headquarters in Nashville as far as advertising and promotion are concerned. Members of Southern Baptist churches have been so indoctrinated by Southern Baptist institutionalism as to be uncomfortable under other religious banners. By way of illustration, in recent years Southern Baptists have made noticeable excursions into those areas which were once considered to be the fields of endeavors of the American Baptist Convention. This unhappy and unnecessary intrusion cannot be explained as a result of protecting or keeping the Southern Baptist faith. As people from the South have moved into these areas, they have missed the "program" — the familiar sights, sounds, and smells — of Southern Baptist churches. To some extent they have asked the Southern Baptist Convention to invade uncommon territories and to establish churches in those areas. In most instances, doctrine and liturgy have not been even a small part of the question. "Once Southern Baptists always Southern Baptists" seems to be a more accurate explanation. This is extreme institutionalism, and it is part and parcel of the success of Southern Baptists across the country.

At the same time, Southern Baptists have maintained a decided sectarian flavor in their churches. They think in concepts of new birth, baptism by the Holy Spirit, individual and personal religion, and rewards in heaven. They believe that society can change for the better only as individuals are converted and saved by the gospel. They recognize the authority of the Scriptures and look to the Holy Spirit for their illumination.

It is unfair and inaccurate to suggest that their otherworldly emphases are a means of comforting them in their prejudices. More likely, it comforts them when their prejudices are brought to the surface and they are traumatized by the fact of judgment and the necessity for change. They are not hopelessly mired in the impossible task of making this a perfect world. Their stake is in the transcendent promise of an eternal kingdom whose boundaries are not identical with the limits of time and space.

INCARNATIONAL STYLE

To suggest that the church must be a sectarian institution is to demand that it have an incarnational style. From the moment that "the Word became flesh and dwelt among us, full of grace and truth" (John 1:14), the incarnational style of the church was set in motion. It was confirmed with the event of the resurrection. The church is the "body of Christ." No other symbol is needed to convince that its style is that of incarnation.

In this respect, it is evident that the Roman Catholic church adopted the incarnational style from the very first. It sees itself as the vicar of Christ through the papal office. It purports to be a trustee of Christ in his absence. Subsequent to the ascension, the Roman church has conceived of itself as taking the place of Christ and fulfilling his function in history. "The Church — an extension of the incarnation" — is essentially its own descriptive phrase. Germane to the premise under consideration is that the church with the most decided incarnational style is also the most highly institutionalized of all religious bodies.

Despite its obvious commitment to religious institution, the Roman Catholic combination of incarnation and institution is unacceptable. In virtually replacing Christ in history, it gives minimal significance to the resurrection. It rules out the possibility of the risen Lord acting on the planes of history. It contradicts its most descriptive phrase. It cannot be an extension of the incarnation because the incarnate One is replaced by the church itself. In short, it gives too little room to the "sectarian Jesus."

Every sectarian corrective has been too extreme. In their aversion to Roman Catholicism, the sectarians have declared for churches that are no more than bodies of believers. Roman Catholics so institutionalized Christ as to hide him beneath a welter of their own authoritarian presumptions. Religious sects have been so busy pointing to Jesus as to keep him outside their institutions and locked up in their own personal pilgrimages of faith. From their beginnings until now, sectarians have appealed only to those who have shared their own experiences of faith. The prospective convert has not been able to find Jesus in the sectarians' churches. He must somehow make his way into the interior realms of the sectarians' personal faith. While this sectarian stance has created enthusiastic fellowships of believers, it has failed to provide the enduring qualities of institutions. The sectarian movements of the sixteenth and seventeenth centuries were originally characterized by a great sense of unity. The characteristics of religious institutions were largely ignored for the sake of being one in Christ. It is ironic but not surprising that these same groups proved to be capable of the most grievous kinds of religious hostility and division. This can only add up to their failure to institutionalize their faith to any comprehensive degree.

In comparison with the more established churches, sectarian bodies have a very narrow theory of incarnation. The former denominations believe that the Presence is not only in individuals but in believing communities and in the sacraments. Sectarians confine the incarnation to embodiment exclusively in the individual, in the heart or soul of the person. It is significant that the more incarnational churches are more highly institutionalized. Less incarnational churches are inclined to give institution very little status.

The problem before the church of today is how to be incarnational in style and institutional in nature without smothering the Spirit within its body and without making Christ relatively dispensable. This will call for some scriptural and theological insights into incarnation which do not come from the mind of the apostle Paul. His gift of incarnational metaphors describing the church is still unexcelled. "The new creation," "household of God," "bride of Christ," and the magnificent "body of Christ" are tremendous symbols.

Unfortunately, Paul's theology of the incarnation falls far short of his poetry. The cross and the resurrection are the dominant themes of Paul's thought. The life and teachings of Jesus furnish a context for his treatment of the atonement. In his doctrine, the God of Christ on the cross towers above the God of Christ in history.

Paul thought of the church as a suffering and dying instrument despite his admonitions to build up the body. As for Philippians 2, deemed by many to be an incarnational hymn, I am inclined to agree with D. M. Baillie that this interpretation mistakes "its poetry for theological theory." The kenotic theory (self-emptying) arising out of this Scripture does little to enhance the concept of incarnation:

> For though the Son of God thus keeps His personal identity in becoming the subject of human attributes which He assumes, He has divested Him-

self of the *distinctively divine attributes;* which would imply, if language means anything, that in becoming human He ceased to be divine.[4]

An excursion into the Gospel of John may supply the answers we seek. To be sure, the Fourth Gospel is not an exhaustive document on ecclesiology. But there can be no question as to the importance it places on the incarnation. Nor is there any cause to believe that its incarnational tones cannot resound in the symphonies of the church.

In addition to that opening crescendo, "and the Word became flesh" (John 1:14), are such reminders as "I am the vine, you are the branches" (John 15:5). This means that the church bears the fruit of the work of the Incarnate One only as it is, at any time and always, inseparable from him. The prayer of Christ that his company be in but not of the world means that the church is an institution in the kingdom not of this world as well as being an institution in culture. The risen Lord is not trapped in the sacraments of Roman Catholicism. Neither is he imprisoned in the individual soul. He is head of the body, a people who dwell in him and in whom he dwells for the redemption of history and the final vindication of his righteousness when history runs out of breath.

THE SPHERES OF THE SACRED AND THE PROFANE

The church cannot be a sectarian institution until it manages to recover two spheres of human existence: the profane and the sacred. The first sphere refers to a realm which is not self-consciously set apart for the redemptive mission of God in the world. The second refers to that realm which has been set apart for mission and has accepted its burden.

The unquestionable benefits of worldly religion and a secularized gospel are now subject to the law of diminishing returns. Religion in general, worldly religion, coffee-house dialogue, evangelism by indirection, and theology in the marketplace have all had their day. It is now time for the saints to go back to the temple.

Worldly religion is a product of the failure of religious institutions to be sectarian and the refusal of religious sects to be institutionalized.

The least sectarian of all religious institutions is obviously the Roman Catholic church. It is not coincidence that it is also the most parochial of all religious bodies. As a result, it has consistently enlarged its parish by means of its related institutions. It has expected its schools and its hospitals to foster and to keep the Roman Catholic faith. In other words, Roman Catholic institutions, although not designed to be the church, have been burdened with the mission of the church.

Other major denominations have tagged along in this way. By establishing and maintaining church-related institutions, they have endeavored to spread their influence through culture. These parochial endeavors originally enjoyed an abundant success. Present trends suggest that these successes are now winding down to an ignominious halt. Denominations of every kind, including Roman Catholicism, are severing their relationships with the schools and hospitals they brought into existence. Inability to meet the financial needs of these institutions is the most obvious cause for separation. Beneath these surface reasons lies the hard reality that church-related institutions have not fulfilled the expectations of their creators. They have not been able to keep the faith which their churches leased out to them.

Even sectarian bodies have not been able to protect their related institutions from the inroads of secularism. Oral Roberts, who founded the Oral Roberts University, has given evidence of this fact. In all innocence he has recently announced that the most wonderful and exciting event to be imagined has happened at his school. One might expect this to be in the nature of a campus-wide revival or a visitation of the Spirit. Not at all; the most wonderful event is that the university has been accredited. That accreditation has not come from God but from a very secular association.

It could not have turned out otherwise in the long run.

Schools and hospitals are not churches. They cannot do the work of churches. They can do only the work of schools and hospitals. A hospital is not the "body of Christ." *Pro humanitates* is not inevitably synonymous with "Christ is Lord." Whenever the church presumes to transplant Christ into a related institution, it has forgotten Who is head of the body.

Sectarians have brought on secular usurpations with equal force. They have accomplished it in a different way. Jesus has been captive in their hearts rather than in ecclesiastical bodies. Disavowing the boundaries and precincts of the sacred, they have presumed to impose their religious experiences upon people in all kinds of situations. Usually armed with "Jesus" and their Bibles, they have tried to change the world through one-to-one evangelism. Little notice has been given to the shape of society. Distinctions between the blighted people of the ghetto and the affluent ones of suburbia have hardly been taken into account. They practice what Berger has suggested is ill-advised. And they are now discovering that all such attempts to maintain one's own counterdefinitions of the world are virtually impossible and wind up in the "nightmare *par excellence.*" (See p. 59.)

There is no more transcendence in a Jesus Christ within the human heart than in a Jesus Christ trapped in sacrament and institution. In either instance Christ tends to be interpreted as a follower of men rather than men being followers of Christ. Christ has come to his people for the sake of the world. But he has not and does not come to the world willy-nilly. Neither the world, nor its institutions, nor the individual person is the body of Christ. The church is the body of Christ.

THE LORD'S DAY

The tale of what has happened to Sunday in our culture illustrates the need for the recovery of the sacred and the profane spheres.

As a first chapter, it should be realized that the church,

as a religious institution, had to discover and secure its own time and place in history. Conceived in the incarnation, it was born of the resurrection and has been nurtured by its hope for the Parousia. Parousia means both *presence* and *coming*. Neville Clark is illuminating:

> Once more it is true that the Messiah is not without his people. Already they are risen with Christ: this is the present reality. At the last, they will appear with Christ: this is the future hope. . . . The goal of history and the fulfilment of expectation is not the "coming" of Jesus.[5]

The goal of history is the *parousia totus Christus*, head and members.

> For the disclosure of the Messiah carries with it the disclosure of the Church; and the glory of both remains concealed to the final Day. . . . It implies no solitary glorification. The Christ comes precisely "to be glorified in his saints."[6]

The church was and is responsible for bearing fruit between the day of resurrection, the reality of our being risen with Christ, and the time of the Parousia, the hope of our being glorified with Christ. Clark continues:

> Given this realization, to write off the period between the Resurrection and the coming of Christ was impossible. The interim was not a hiatus. It was a period filled with redemptive activity. Therefore it was no longer sufficient to think and live solely in terms of "the third day" and "the last day."[7]

Having seized upon this day in history for its proclamation, the church confronted the culture of the Western world with what it should do with Sunday. The world made considerable accommodation, and it became a day of rest and worship.

As it has turned out, society has neither the mind nor the muscle for celebrating Sunday. At the present time Sunday is more a day for diversion than for rest from labor and as a day of worship. It has lost its status as a social institution.

Begrudging that loss, the church has wasted time and energy trying to withstand an almost irreversible trend. Believing that it is being overwhelmed by secularism, the church tends to thwart its own efforts to stem the tide by insisting that society keep Sunday sacrosanct. This only adds to the process of its secularization.

The church should never have given Sunday over to society in the first place. Culture is not designed to keep the Sunday faith. The Lord's Day is a religious institution rather than a social institution. It cannot be celebrated outside the temple in the sphere of the profane. It belongs within the sphere of the sacred.

Trends indicate that the time is not far off when worshipers will have to make their way to churches through throngs of shoppers and vacationers. Eventually the church will proclaim the Lord's Day as an institution that is set apart from the culture in which it lives. This will also contribute to the recovery of the sacred boundaries of life in which the religious institution is at home and from which it can make its mission to the world.

8. On Becoming a Sectarian Institution

The suggestion that the church should become a sectarian institution flirts with improbability. Sectarian and ecclesiastical styles of the churches have always existed side by side throughout religious history. But they have given no promise of mixing with any greater facility than oil and water.

A plausible concept of what a sectarian institution ought to be may go far to assure that it can become a reality. In this respect the life-style of the sectarian institution may be conceptualized by four major characteristics: joyful reactionism, justification by Christ alone, celebration, and inclusiveness. It is possible for the church to realize itself both as an institution and a sect if it emphasizes these facets of its nature.

Implicit in the blend of these life-styles are some of the distinctive characteristics of the ecclesiastical and sectarian features of the church. In fact, joyful reactionism includes both in a single category. As an institution the church lives because of what has happened as well as because of what it expects or hopes to happen. It deals with given realities by acting on the *a priori* of the kingdom of God ushered into history with the coming of Jesus Christ. Its reactionary style may be described as response to the new without undue alacrity or celerity. The church knows that nothing that is new is necessarily or inevitably any better than what it already has.

The sectarian nature of the church spices its institutional reactionism with the quality of joy. For the church cannot be content merely with depending on its traditional verities. It must know how to celebrate them. We do not celebrate what is yet to be. We celebrate that which has already come to pass. The author of First John offers a superb text for joyful reactionism: "Beloved, we are God's children now; it does not yet appear what we shall be, but we know that when he appears we shall be like him, for we shall see him as he is" (1 John 3:2).

In the second place, a sectarian institution should be in the world without sensing any obligation to pay the world for its existence. Christ justifies its presence, and it need not look to the world for justification. This goes against the grain of current moods. They contain the suggestion that the church must serve the world in order to justify its existence. In this view, the church has no right to be concerned with itself; it must only be concerned for the world. Both sides of this issue are to be found in Psalm 122 along with a surprising and dynamic answer.

When the pilgrim author of this psalm had celebrated the Feast of Thanksgiving at the temple in Jerusalem, he emerged with a prayer for the peace and the prosperity of the city. Having gone with gladness to the "house of the Lord," he experienced a poetic concern for the city which embraced the house. This is surely "grist for the mill" of the despisers of the institutional church. The pilgrim went to the church, but his chief concern was for the city of man. That seems to have been the essence of his prayer song. What a boon this is for the advocates of worldly religion! Here is their text enjoining man to leave the church and to intercede for the secular city. As they see it, the church cannot otherwise be justified. They would do well to take a longer look at Psalm 122. That last line explains the psalmist's loving concern for Jerusalem:

> For the sake of the house of the Lord our God,
> I will seek your good.   Psalm 122:9

Some if not most of his love for Jerusalem was because it was the home of the temple.

As a sectarian institution, the church will be more of a celebrator than a problem solver. This is not to say that the church should have no concern for social problems. I cannot imagine how it could have self-respect unless it were concerned. But its basic life-style should not be so much that of a problem solver as that of a celebrator.

The church's success in meeting social needs will depend in large measure upon its capacity for celebration. The manner in which it attacks the particular problems of its time will be affected no little by whether or not it feels that the universal problem has already been solved. I suppose it is safe to suggest that humanism believes that man is both the universal question and the universal answer. The Christian faith, on the other hand, agrees that man is the universal question but vigorously denies that he is the universal answer. The death and resurrection of Jesus Christ is the universal answer. In this respect the answer has already been given. Only as the church celebrates this reality is it prepared to sally forth into the world with its problem-solving kit. It would not and should not have the heart for that mission under other conditions.

Unfortunately, a liquor firm beat the pulpit to putting this theme into colorful words. An advertisement praising a particular brand of liquor has it like this:

> It is not for solving problems.
> It is for celebrating solutions.

There may be little or no difference between getting drunk because one has problems and because one has solved his problems as far as liquor is concerned. But there is a world of difference between getting "anxiously drunk" and "spiritually drunk" as far as Christian celebration is concerned. In fact, Christians are encouraged to get drunk on the Spirit.

As the sacred community pulls back from parochialism, it should adopt more of an inclusive life-style than it has had for centuries. As it refuses to go as far away from home as it once did in order to engage man at the secular junctures of life, it must be more tolerant of those who may come looking for it. Rather than continuing to enlarge its parochial circle, the church must now begin to experiment with widening its gates and lowering its fences and increasing its number of entrances. The end of parochialism should never mean a diminishment of the accessibility of the church. Whoever wishes to join with the sacred community must not find formidable barriers in his path.

The church can afford radical openness if its style reflects a redeeming community instead of one redeemed. The features of a regenerate church membership ought to be discarded. They have never really fitted the church from the beginning. Ecclesiologists of the established churches will quite obviously have less trouble with this transformation than will their sectarian counterparts. Infant baptism has always hinted at the need and justification of an inclusive church. But the corresponding act of confirmation has been an ill-advised corrective. Although I am not an advocate of infant baptism, I am in sympathy with that part of the established church which contends that confirmation is not necessary for authenticating whatever has happened in infant baptism. Most certainly confirmation should not be used as a *final filter* to filter out what already has been taken in.

Sectarian figures, usually enamored with the implications of believer's baptism, are not as likely to cotton to an inclusive church. If their rigid stance is to mean anything, however, they are obligated to assure that the baptism of believers only always transpires. There are quite legitimate doubts that this can ever be sufficiently proven.

Everything depends, in this context, on the church's capacity for being redemptive with its own people. If its redeeming power is beamed only to the unchurched, then every church member must obviously be redeemed before he joins. But if the church dares to believe that something, redemptive and powerful in its scope, happens to its people after they are churched, then the church can throw away many of its filters.

TOWARD JOYFUL REACTIONISM

If the church is to achieve a joyful reactionism, it will have to learn how to laugh at its reactionary tendencies. I have already suggested that the church responds to all things in light of that which has already happened: the coming of the kingdom with Jesus and assurances of that kingdom in his death and resurrection.

A healthy sectarian institution will have a sense of humor about all this. If the church cannot see the humor in its uneasiness with its own reactionism, it is lost. It does not really want to be reactionary. It is intrigued by those who purportedly live on the cutting edges. But it smiles at the realization that when the cutting edge gets crowded, it loses much of its keenness. The church would prefer to live on the first horizon, so that it could dip into the sun's red hues and finger paint the clouds. It wants to be with it: "to dig," to be "hip," and "to be where the action is." The church listens intently to its critics, particularly its bright young clergy who carp about its irrelevance and take its temperature and feel its pulse. They are religion's holy hypochondriacs.

The church must realize that, if this is the way of relevance, it must play at being church. It has to play at being church as if the game is more authentic than the purported reality. It must wager that this is the case. Churchmen ought to disagree with the Sunday school teacher who tacked this notice on the bulletin board of her room: "Children, this is God's house. Do not clown in here." Would that God's house had many more clowns! It would be at once more real and more fun. Jesus did not seem pleased because there were too few clowns in his generation. Matthew 11:16 indicates his loneliness because the people refused to play at weddings or funerals and decided that John had a demon and that Jesus was an alcoholic.

The church can live with its joyful reactionism to the extent of its willingness to forgo relevance for the sake of true value. In its more recent past, it has discarded what may have been truly valuable for the less valuable when that appeared to be more relevant. The irony of it all is that the church has always believed it had a supportive text for doing so. The parable of the old garment and old wineskins has been mutilated by virtue of this kind of misconstruction. The parable has been customarily interpreted as making a case for the impossibility of combining the old with the new. Since what is new is invariably linked with what is relevant, the old has suffered accordingly.

There is a better and more useful interpretation which provides a necessary fundamental for deciding when to keep what is old and when to discard it. All of us need some such index if we are to maintain our equilibrium in the precarious posture of the present. That posture is always tilting us toward the side of the new. The parable affords a chance for better balance.

If the old and the new are unfailingly incompatible, which is to take precedence over the other? To which do we assign priority? Stripped naked of all other considerations, a decision to discard the old for the new is almost inevitable. This can reach the point of being ridiculous.

We may confidently assume that Jesus never bothered about being relevant. His own mission was so radically new that he did not have to bother. I am convinced, however, that he would not have bothered even if the situation had been otherwise. In any event, this parable has more to do with value and its priority than with the priorities of relevance.

Consider an old garment that is still worthy of being repaired. Is any piece of patch cloth, no matter how new it is, of more value than the whole garment? Of course it is not. Under these circumstances it would be foolish to destroy the garment's remaining usefulness with a new patch that would tear it all the more. So the church with all good humor must not submit to repair with new patches which will rend it to pieces. It is far better for the church to wear a few tatters and make jokes about them.

On the other hand, new wine is of more value than are old wineskins. Even a Baptist knows that much. The potential maturity of new wine should never be jeopardized by containers that cannot preserve it until it has reached its ultimate flavor.

Taken in this light, the church cannot always afford to be reactionary. It must have a capacity for receiving new truth and new means of its expression. On the other hand, like a tattered clown, it must sometimes be smilingly content with what it has.

TO HIM WHO GIVES IT LIFE

It is very hard for the church to be in the world without feeling obligated to the world. The increasing pressure to enact laws that will tax the church is a case in point. Many of these nit-picking debates center around the doctrine of the separation of church and state. Without discounting the considerable merits of this categorical argument, I do not think that it is central to the present issue.

Without the growing conviction that the church owes society something like rent for its place in the world, the debate would never have gotten off the ground. If and when the church is taxed, totally and indiscriminately, it can only mean that we have come to the day when Americans are convinced that the church must be forced to pay its way. Parenthetically, I think all profit-making enterprises of organized religion should be taxed. That position stems from the conviction that the church is not being itself when it gets into the money-making game. But when it is being the church — nothing more or else — it owes the world nothing because it does not depend on the world for its life and being.

The church is primarily and ultimately obligated to him who has called it into being. And that is Jesus Christ alone. Perhaps the most popular text of the preachers of the ancient church was from Psalm 118:

> The stone which the builders rejected
> has become the head of the corner.
> This is the Lord's doing;
> it is marvelous in our eyes.
> This is the day which the Lord has made;
> let us rejoice and be glad in it.

What the world discarded then and still discards has become the cornerstone of the church. It is Jesus Christ who supports the church and who holds it together. He has gathered it from out of the world for his purpose. He is the focus of the church's obligation. It owes everything to him and to none other.

Although the church should have its own life-style, it must be the first to realize that it does not have a life of its own. Its life is the living Lord. That is symbolized by the use of unleavened bread in the liturgy of Jewish and Christian communities of faith. For the Jew, as the ancient Feast of Unleavened Bread became connected with the Passover, the bread "commemorated the haste in which Israel left Egypt." There was not time for leaven to do its work. Deeper and more profound than this in Jewish worship is the fact that the sacrifices of men to God should be without leaven. God is his own strength and vitality. He has no need for the energy of leavened bread.

This theme is not lost to the Christian Eucharist or Communion as far as the use of unleavened bread is concerned. However, the use of Communion wine may have a counterbalancing effect to its most distinctive meaning.

Unleavened bread in the Eucharist reminds the Christian that new life is not vested in the sacrifice, neither as he gives it nor takes it into himself. It reminds him that life is vested in a crucified and risen Lord who is the "bread of life."

> Your fathers ate the manna in the wilderness, and they died. This is the bread which comes down from heaven, that a man may eat of it and not die. I am the living bread which came down from heaven; if any one eats of this bread, he will live for ever; and the bread which I shall give for the life of the world is my flesh (John 6:49-51).

As for the use of wine, I have frequently poked fun at those of us who celebrate the Lord's Supper with unfermented juice. I am now forced to take some second thoughts. It appears that we have been doing the right thing for the wrong reasons. The aversion of some Christian moralists to any form of alcohol lies behind this practice in most places. There is a far better reason as I now see it. Unfermented juice may serve the same purpose as unleavened bread. Man's vitality is not supplied by what he gives in sacrifice. Leaven and wine are the work of Christ. The symbols that are without life are given life by the resurrection of our Lord.

To whatever degree the church recognizes and understands these realities, it will know that its obligation for life and being is not to the world but to its Lord.

THE NATURE OF CELEBRATION

The church will have to concentrate on two things if it is to learn the art of celebration. In the first place, it must maintain a usable past as well as assure a usable future. As has already been observed, celebration must use the materials of what has already occurred. If the church has no usable past — a usable past must be both recoverable and valuable — it will have nothing to celebrate.

There are a number of requirements to this end of maintaining a usable past. Let me mention only the most important one. A worthy tradition is one of the means by which the church may have a recoverable and usable past. By its very definition, tradition is a link with the past, providing continuity between present and past realities.

Tradition must not be confused with nostalgia. Nostalgia represents a longing for an irrecoverable past that borders on neurosis. Sometime ago I took my wife, my two married daughters, and their children to see an elderly aunt. I had not visited her for years, and my grandchildren had never been to her home in the Kentucky hill country.

One of my daughters was on a weight-reduction program at the time. On the way down I said to her, "If my aunt bakes some lemon pies for dinner, you must go off your diet for this one time and eat a slice of that pie." I explained to her that it was old-fashioned lemon pie the likes of which could no longer be found anywhere else. To my great delight I discovered soon after our arrival that lemon pie was the dessert for the day.

All of us ate the pie with great relish. My daughter assured me that my praise was not extravagant. She agreed that she had never tasted better lemon pie. Then my wife asked for the recipe and that was the introduction to a tragedy. Initially, it turned out that my aunt had not even baked those pies. They were the handiwork of her eldest daughter and my first cousin, who had come to be with us at dinner. Had my wife been content with that small catastrophe, the day would not have been a total disaster. But she was not to be dissuaded. She asked my cousin for the recipe. And my cousin began, "First of all, you go to the store and get some lemon jello pudding. . . ." I could not bear to hear the rest, and for a day following I suffered nostalgic indigestion, which my wife and children did nothing to alleviate.

A good tradition is built by doing the right thing at the right time with a view to preserving its values. In other words, tradition is a matter of living fully in the present. If the church is too concerned about the past or future at any given time in its history, it may militate against its chances for a rich tradition. There is little worth remembering about the past other than what was done in the right way at the right time. These events, so very timely in their given situations, have a way of becoming germane to other years as they make their way into the present.

The second requirement in learning the art of celebration

involves a modification of the church's definitions and practices of love. Christians have adopted too grim a view of the meaning of love. When the word *"agape"* was picked up by the early Christians because it was an ambiguous word, it provided a counterbalance for the excesses of the concept of *eros*. The latter, simply defined, meant love for what was attractive. At the time, the ideas of *eros* may have needed some restraint. This is no longer the case. So intent have Christians been to make sure that they loved the unattractive that they now are suspicious of their motives if they love what attracts them. We have been so brainwashed as to be afraid to enjoy what we love. Karl Barth understood the nature of the problem:

> The Greeks with their *eros*—and it was no inconsiderable but a very real achievement—grasped the fact that the being of man is free, radically open, willing, spontaneous, joyful, cheerful and gregarious. . . . Yet for all that the Greeks were able to reveal the human heart, to show what humanity is in itself and as such even in a state of distortion and corruption, to bring out the enduring factor in humanity which persists in spite of distortion and corruption, in a way which cannot be said of any other ancient people (and especially Israel, the people of God), and which can to some extent be said of the peoples of later Western history only as and because they have learned concerning *eros* from the ancient Greeks. How these Greeks knew to see themselves as men, to speak with one another, to live together in freedom, as friends, as teachers and scholars, and above all as citizens! [1]

In taking note of the setting in which Paul made use of *eros*, Barth had this to say:

> The theology of Paul and his proclamation of Christian love derives neither from the Greeks nor the barbarians but from Israel. But when he portrays the Christian living in this love he never uses barbarian or Israelitish colours and contours, but he undoubtedly makes use of Greek, thus betraying the fact that he both saw and took note of the Greeks and their *eros*.[2]

The Christian community must, of course, have the will and the capacity to love everyone. It cannot pick and choose in this respect. It is under command to offer *agape* to all men. At the same time, the living out of Christian love in the sectarian institution ought to take on the manner of *eros*. There can otherwise be no celebration.

We encourage people by loving them unequivocally. We

compliment them by enjoying them. This kind of joy is the stuff of celebration in the church. And why not? It is not considered inappropriate to enjoy the rest of God's handiwork. We are not criticized for our enjoyment of a flower's fragrance or the taste of a spring breeze, or for the delight of cooling our feet in a brook. We are free to be gourmets of fine foods: new potatoes, spring peas, leg of lamb, old ham, steak, butterscotch pie, and even spinach. In these ways we celebrate the creation of God. Since the person, himself, is creation's crown, we are not only free but obligated to enjoy each other. Such is a tragically uncommon occurrence. As a usual thing, when a young couple parts after a date, each says to the other, "I enjoyed *it*." For some reason — maybe the influence of *agape* — they seldom say, "I enjoyed *you*."

The enjoyment of God's gift of his people each to the other is the occasion for celebration. For he has given us life, abundant and eternal, in the presence of one another.

REMOVING THE FINAL FILTER

It has already been hinted that the establishmentarian side of the sectarian institution is its best hope for being inclusive. To that end, therefore, the institutional nature of the church must be highlighted. Even in this respect, care should be taken to guard against an extreme imbalance. The late Paul Tillich used just the right words in this regard. He wrote:

> ... a church is a community of those who affirm that Jesus is the Christ. The very name "Christian" implies this. For the individual, this means a decision—*not* as to whether he, personally, can accept the assertion that Jesus is the Christ, *but* the decision as to whether he wishes to belong or not to belong to a community which asserts that Jesus is the Christ.[3]

Tillich's view clashes with both the sectarian and the institutional segments of the church. It differs with the pedobaptist intimations of the established church. Infant baptism suggests that church membership is not dependent upon the decision of the individual. It parts company with the sectarian emphasis upon the authentic church as a body of believing and regenerate persons. Despite his disagreement with these polarities, Tillich described the essence of an inclusive sectarian institution.

The church is a community proclaiming that Jesus is the Christ and Christ is Lord. The membership of the community should be comprised of those who make a responsible and accountable decision to join. This is Tillich's polemic against pedobaptist membership.

Some of the members will find it possible to accept the assertion that Jesus is the Christ as an element of their own personal belief. Others will not be able to do this but may still want to belong to a community making such a proclamation. These people should also be included. This is Tillich's polemic against the sectarian emphasis on a believing and regenerate membership.

In this setting the church will be forced to become a redemptive community. That is to say that it will concentrate on being redeeming rather than redeemed. No longer can it insist on absolute and unequivocal personal belief as the condition for membership.

New methods of incorporating church members will be necessary for actualizing this kind of sacred community. Profession of faith by baptism, infant baptism and confirmation, and transfer by letter will continue to have their place. But transfer by letter should encompass every denomination of the church. No Christian should be excluded from one community because of a difference of dogma in his former community of faith. Not only should there be open membership, but dual membership ought also to become the practice. Given the mobility of modern man, it should be possible for an individual to belong to more than one church even of different denominations with all rights and responsibilities pertaining thereto.

The church must eventually face the question about "unbelievers" in its midst. This is, of course, contingent on the fact of their personal decisions to belong. Do unbelievers not have as much right to be in a world of believers as do believers have the right to be in a world of unbelievers? I am convinced that the church should work redemptively within its community as well as in the world. And it desperately needs to learn more about doing the former.

9. The Need of a Dramatizing Presence

Christians should think of themselves as a dramatizing presence in history. They should be actors before the world's audience. And they should act out God's redemptive love for all men. The basic distinction between Christians and other people is not that the former are "saved" and the others are "lost." The difference is that the former are the actors and the latter make up the audience. Jesus calls all men to receive the gift of salvation. He selects particular men to be his disciples, dramatizing God's redemptive powers for all who will come and see.

The script of this drama is unique. It does not read that unless men profess and become Christian, they cannot be saved; unless men profess and become Christian, they cannot be his disciples. In radical terms the script reveals that one does not have to be a Christian in order to be the object of God's gracious mercy. It is the role of the Christian to act out this truth in behalf of those who are not Christian. In short the script reads: "You do not have to be a Christian to receive God's grace." The beautiful paradox is that only the Christian is selectively equipped to know and to say this to his fellowmen.

Of no little importance is the stage on which this drama primarily takes place. Although the show must sometimes go "on the road," it is not basically a road show. The religious edifice is the chief stage, and worship is the most congenial setting.

Although no one could easily accuse Howard Moody of belonging to the establishment, he seems to agree with my conclusions about the primary place for the drama. Moody carries on a remarkably innovative ministry at Judson Memorial Church in Greenwich Village, New York City. What he has to say, somewhat inadvertently, about the place of the drama is all the more intriguing.

> It is significant that *the Church happens in a space or place*. For some time, during the anti-building kick which accompanied the recovery of the truth that the Church is people, we felt very guilty about our Romanesque, rambling old brickpile. At times we were ashamed not to have sold it and "gone on the road," but as we saw *mission* "happen" here we realized that the church must happen in a place or space. To deny this is to raise a serious question about the reality of the Incarnation. When the Church becomes a reality it is incarnate, visible, concrete, occupying a certain space at a certain time.[1]

This is where the drama must first take place. Only after the church has become a theater of salvation may it "go on the road" with sufficient confidence to put on a good show. The fact that it can put on a better show in its accustomed surroundings and with better props will not excuse its failure to take its drama to the people. But it must not be premature in this matter. It must wait until it has worked through the setting, script, and cast. Nor can it stay on the road incessantly. There must be a base to which it can return. Its initial opening is for those who can and will come to the church for the redemptive drama. As for the rest of the people, it goes to them gladly and at the proper time well prepared to put on the show.

A PROBLEM WITH UNSELFCONSCIOUSNESS

Not until the church consciously tries to be a dramatizing presence will it succeed in putting on the right kind of show. Not too long ago I saw two students, of opposite sex, playing a steamed-up, extremely intimate, and modern version of "post office" in front of the university's post office. Knowing that I should neither stare nor in any other way lose my composure, I nonchalantly went about the business of mailing a letter. Upon my return the two were still there, impervious to everything other than their own mutuality. I inwardly was displeased with their impropriety. My middle-aged reflexes prompted me to view their display of public passion with a bit of asperity. By the time I had reached my office, another insight had impressed me. The two were not aware of their public display. It did not occur to them that they were on stage in front of the crowds milling around the post office. Their interlock had locked out the rest of the world.

The church is capable of a similar imperviousness. It practices its rituals of faith, its symbols of love, and its liturgy of adoration in public view. It does not try to hide anything. Yet it seems unaware that its faith and practice are on stage.

If the church ever had one, it may now be assumed that it has lost its stage presence. The church does not realize that it should be putting on a big show. And it has no idea of how to do that if and when it decides that it should. The church is so concerned with itself, as was the case with the couple, that it has forgotten how to act. Its current debates over matters of form, liturgy, homiletics, jazz and folk masses, sacraments, and the like are quibbles over improving the interior and private life of the church.

As the church decides, and surely it must decide, to become even more open to the world, the necessity for its becoming a self-conscious actor will be all the more pressing. Although the church is a community set apart from the world, it must not hide from the world. It must be radically open to all who will enter, and its total experience must be available to those who want to engage in it.

ON REFUSING TO PLAY

Here again the church must run the risk of hypocrisy. It has already been argued that risking hypocrisy is no easy task for the church. Stung severely by its critics on this matter, it can hardly take up role playing and the wearing of masks with appreciable ease. So much has been said about the hypocrisy of Christians as to make them quite conscience stricken about the entire affair. This may be the reason for the church's surging enchantment with encounter groups or their facsimilies. Among other ambitions, encounter groups encourage their participants to get rid of all their masks. They must be done with role playing and encounter each other as exactly what they are. It is questionable whether this complete unmasking is possible. What may really occur at encounter-group meetings is that people may be shedding dishonest masks and putting on honest ones.

Even if unmasking were completely possible, there is no assurance that the maneuver is an undiluted good. Role playing for the sake of others is much to be commended. Ingar Bergman's "hypocritical pastor" in the film *Winter Light* reveals the nuances in the total issue. Having lost his faith at the death of his wife, the pastor tried to avoid the request of a young mother that he should counsel with her depressed husband. Being unsuccessful in his evasion, he had to meet the man on a Sunday afternoon following a worship service which had left him empty and washed up. Upon finally confronting his distressed parishioner, the pastor could no longer contain himself. He became the patient in the conversation. He poured out the doubts and despair of his own soul in a torrential confession. Finally, the parishioner pulled himself loose from his pastor's imploring grasp and fled from the church. Shortly thereafter he committed suicide.

The pastor visited the bereaved widow and departed with the knowledge that he had been of no comfort to her. He had yet another crisis to face. The time for evening vespers was near. Should he continue to play the role of preacher and priest, or should he tear away his mask and go honest before the world? He finally appeared at the church with great reluctance. No one was there except the drunken organist, a devoted mistress for whom he cared next to nothing, and the old arthritic custodian. The latter sensed the mood of the pastor without knowing its cause. He tried to buoy him up by observing that when the church bell struck the hour, the parishioners would come to worship. The bell tolled out its invitation. No one else came. Then the pastor made his decision. He climbed into the high pulpit and intoned the words of glory to God.

He kept on his mask and he played his role. Was he an unspeakable hypocrite? In a sense he was certainly a hypocrite. But he may have remembered what occurred in the wake of complete honesty. A man had possibly taken his own life as a result of that. No one can be certain what Bergman intended in this drama. As for me, I came away from it believing that the pastor had achieved one of his finest hours.

As the first actors in Greek drama wore their masks, so must Christians of our time be willing to do likewise. The show must go on. I do not expect an easy or immediate acceptance of this view. Perhaps the reader will reject the premise completely. The extent of such rejection will reflect the church's unreadiness to be a dramatizing presence.

The church has forgotten how to play. It knows next to nothing about turning tragedy over to the irrepressible laughter of comedy. It no longer knows how to pretend, how to engage in festivity, and how to tinker with fantasy. It has lost the script, which is written in transcendent moods that are never to be captured completely by worldly realism. It takes itself entirely too seriously. As a result, it no longer teaches us how to laugh in the face of tragedy but only to giggle as we are reduced to ashes.

AN UNFUNNY THING HAPPENED AT THE GAME

Secular institutions give little promise of dramatizing our history, of bringing elements of play into our existence so that we may make a game out of life. Only the church seems to have that ability, and it is not now using it. Life grows grimmer as the church consistently fails to meet this need.

As but one example, consider the problem of competition, especially in Western society. Competition grinds away at individuals until they are broken and defeated. It lies behind the evils of poverty, race discrimination, political corruption, and war. Many people are concerned for the future if the competitive motif in culture goes unchecked and even unchallenged. Proposed solutions are unfortunately a study in naïveté and innocence. Cooperation is simplistically suggested as an alternative for competition. Love and understanding as the media for all relationships are offered as a cure-all. It apparently has not occurred to most of these innocent proposers that such recommendations have no chance at all in the competitive jungle of life.

No matter how much modern man is repelled by relentless competition, it is a fact of his life. Ours is not the first generation to be concerned with the power of competition and its meaning. Surely the Genesis authors must have been wondering why man had to struggle in order to eke out a mere existence from the stubborn earth. Somehow they realized that the unyielding ground was a result of man's rebellion before God. And this is what they wrote:

> Because you . . . have eaten of the tree
> of which I commanded you,
> "You shall not eat of it,"
> cursed is the ground because of you;
> in toil you shall eat of it all the
> days of your life; (Genesis 3:17).

No one has to agree with Genesis in order to recognize that his earthly existence is a very competitive matter. All living things must sustain themselves on the planet Earth as far as we now know. This means that they must eat one another.

Vegetarians, who cannot bring themselves to eat the meat of animals which have been slain, ought to take note of a very apparent reality. Most of the plants they eat come from injured ground. The earth must be cut and gouged by the plow for them to be able to promote their nonviolent philosophy.

Competition is just as much a fact of life in society as it is in the natural world. There is neither time nor space to elaborate upon this premise. It may be only mentioned that the genius of a free nation depends upon parties and persons competing for election to the offices of government. It also seems likely that nations, which diminish competition within their own boundaries, become highly competitive and imperialistic on a worldwide scale. Soviet Russia and Communist China are primary examples.

Furthermore, individuals invariably compete with other individuals in the arena of values. Although they may try to set such competition in a refined category of ideals and ideas only, the nature of man causes him to take ideological victories or defeats so personally as to throw him into the middle of the conflict. In brief, if another person's ideas are as good as one's own, there is no reason to give expression to either one. But if one person's values or ideas are superior to those of another, he is obligated to give them social expression.

Competition is inevitable under the existing circumstances of life. It is also necessary unless we take pains to make a subtle distinction between inevitability and necessity. In either case, competition cannot be replaced. There is no substitute for what is inevitable and necessary, either or both. Contrary action to this principle may be a prelude to disaster.

Such possible disaster may be predicted by a look at what occurs when competition is diminished or eliminated in a competitive game. Human beings are distinct from other animals in their gamesmanship. The probability that we play games as a means of relief from the abrasively erosive results of competition in the raw is a logical assumption. From a theoretical standpoint, the more competitive games reduce the elementary factors to those of human accomplishment. Brawn and skill as well as mental dexterity are emphasized. Chance and destiny are minimized. Games are played within prescribed boundaries and according to certain rules. Officials are given jurisdiction over the game to see that injustices are not committed without due penalty. Everything is designed to allow the full exercise of competition in which its worst potentialities are held to a minimum.

In recent years I have noticed a diminishment of competition in many of our athletic contests. At a recent football game, for example, I became aware of a new chant from the cheering section. In other days when the offensive team was making yardage in the direction of the other team's goal line, the defense's cheering section would cry: "Hold that line! Hold that line!" This was to inspire the troops to dig in and to use extra effort to stop the onrushing opponents. The new chant goes like this: "Hey, hey, fumble, fumble. Hey, hey, fumble, fumble." The implication is clear. When we eliminate competition from a game, we are doomed to the practice of voodoo. We try to put a hex on the opposition. Or it may be that we appeal to the gods to be discriminating in their gifts of grace and to bestow their mercy and favor on our side at the expense of the other. We reintroduce fate and fortune into the contest at the expense of competition. This does not bring cooperation, however, but rather an exercise in witchcraft.

Elimination of competition from the arena of history may have the same consequence. When we can no longer compete or no longer want to compete, we tend to put a curse on the opposition. As has already been indicated, if we want to be creative, we must compete with modern technology. This could be the reason that so many of us are now cursing technology and are seeking a primitive and simplistic life. Politics are often subjected to similar hexes. We may further presume that the increasing number of "evil eyes" now being beamed at intellectual values originate from the faces of those who want to withdraw from intellectual competition.

Many signs point to the disturbing fact that not even our games afford the relief we want and need from the demanding and oppressive burden of competition. We no longer can tolerate competition even in the context of play. At the same time, competition is inevitable and perhaps necessary. No immediately visible exits from the arena of competition are in evidence.

The church does have a game that affords relief and indicates a reason for hope. It is called Communion, Eucharist, or the Lord's Supper. It is not merely a game of cooperation, although that is a part of it. It is a game of reconciliation. It is a kingdom game. It may be played only with kingdom boundaries and by kingdom rules. It is usually played on Sundays. It is Sunday religion which does not always carry over to Monday. Whoever plays this game should realize that this is not the way life is on the planet Earth. It is a foretaste of life in the kingdom of God. Jesus brought it with him. He enjoins us to enjoy a slice of the kingdom in the here and now. The best is yet to be, and the promise is that it will come to pass.

Competitors become priests to one another. Doctors, lawyers, preachers, salesmen, plumbers, mothers, students, and taxicab drivers have no reason to compete with one another. The grace of God is freely given, and we may share its life-giving elements with each other in abundance. Cups run over. Bread gives life. It does not really matter that the moments of reconciliation cannot become the whole of history for now. The game refreshes and renews us. We can live from one cup to the next. And we can toast the time when the game becomes the reality and the reality becomes only a game.

The church's strange reluctance to provide this kind of drama explains its lack of appeal or meaning to modern man. In his view, "church" represents a visit to "Dullsville." That reason is seldom given voice. People feel constrained to give more proper reasons for ignoring or deserting the church. They paradoxically echo the reasons that the church itself construes to be proper and justifiable. They tell us that they defect because the church is irrelevant, hypocritical, theologically extreme, ethically radical, disunified, lacking fellowship, comprised of improper people, or lacking effective and dedicated leadership. These are good and legitimate reasons in part. The fact, frequently suspected but seldom even whispered, is that people steer clear of the church because it is inexpressibly dull. It hands out tickets to boredom. This need not be. Although there is no assurance that people want to go "where the action is," there is some assurance that they will go "where the acting is."

10. Toward Putting on a Good Show

In order to become "salvation actors," Christians will have to give secondary status to being witnesses or examples. The choice need not be absolute. But when the situation and the times are taken into account, the role of the Christian actor is indicated above the other possibilities.

Pushing the idea of witness out of the top spot cannot be done with flippant ease. To the degree that Christ was an historical figure, this concept will never be eliminated. That he was an historical figure is a certainty. As Mircea Eliade has put it: "He had recourse to no miracle to escape from that historicity. . . ."[1]

Witness is also a prime word in the vocabulary of resurrection. Paul took considerable pains to claim apostleship by virtue of being confronted by the risen Christ at a point on the road to Damascus. He made it clear to all who heard him that his apostolic authority was not conferred on him by the original twelve. Thus when Christians speak as witnesses in present times, they are testifying to their personal encounter with the risen Lord. Witness has been and should always remain an honorable and descriptive word in the vocabulary of faith.

Under existing circumstances, however, the word leaves something to be desired. It encourages the excesses of individualism. We can admit to the propriety — even the necessity — of Paul's disclaimer as far as the influence of the original twelve was concerned. This was indigenous to his eventual mission to the Gentiles. The fact persists, nevertheless, that Paul's individualism constituted a major difficulty in those early days. It is not too much to say that as a result of his sense of individual witness prompted by his isolated experience on the road to Damascus no one could tell Paul anything. Barnabas and Simon Peter could have testified to that and many times over.

As it now stands, "witness" does not enhance the quality of corporateness which is indispensable to the contemporary church. It connotes the phenomenon of an isolated voice apart from the structures and forms of the faithful community. It has already been argued that this cannot be the most effective voice to a highly organized and specialized culture such as now exists.

Furthermore, sinner that he is, man tends to exploit his singular witness to his own advantage. He is susceptible to posing as the only reputable witness to be called to testify. He can so easily claim to be the only one who has seen the truth in its unblemished reality. It is inevitable that at least two people will make this selfsame claim. When this occurs, Jesus as the subject of the witness experience is increasingly obscured. The comparative authenticity of the competing witnesses becomes the chief concern. Out of such foolishness has come John R. Rice's condemnation of Billy Graham for being a liberal.

It is less difficult to reduce the status of man as "example." Jesus is our example. It does not then follow that Christians should think too highly of themselves as examples. They must not run the risk of assuming that they are little Christs. The church should make Christ exemplary to contemporary man without making men become substitute examples in his place. In other words, let Christ rather than men be mythologized.

Christians are authentic if and when they are *faithful*.

Whether or not they are *good* is a secondary consideration. Virtue was a chief good in Greek mentality in the days of Christ. And it was He who suggested that only God was good. Faithfulness is primary for Christians. By this is meant the faithful portrayal of God's redemption through Jesus Christ.

A Christian must be very good if he is to be an example. This is fraught with every conceivable difficulty. Not only do the facts suggest that few men, if any, are good enough to be examples; all attempts to that end bring them perilously close to imperious self-righteousness. There are precarious psychological problems to be considered as well. How does any man, who thinks of himself as an example, avoid feeling superior to those for whom he has tried to become a model?

To be faithful, on the other hand, is to make sure that Jesus Christ is not misrepresented by faulty drama. The church has little stake in whether or not its people are better than other people in the sense of their personal goodness. It must take greater pains to assure that its people are better actors than others. Christ is not betrayed when Christians are not as good as they ought to be. Christ is not betrayed when Christians fail to set a proper example. Christ is betrayed when Christians do not faithfully reproduce the drama of his own example.

A DRAMA OF LIFE AND DEATH

At this present juncture, the church must become a dramatizing presence, a corporate actor reliving the redemptive myth in the ongoing of history. Eliade's observations about history and Western man point up the importance of this kind of drama. He tells us that Western man's passion for history is fairly recent, dating from the second half of the last century. This recent affinity for history in our newly secularized Western culture may be the source of modern man's anxiety. Preoccupation with the details of history naturally makes man more conscious of its end. That is death.

Other cultures, Eastern in particular, have no similar degree of historical consciousness. In these communities, death is not so much an end as an initiatory rite into a new mode of being. The pangs of death are actually trials which are preparatory for new being and new existence. In their view, death is not equated with nothingness. This does not imply that the East has no sense of history. They believe to live in history is good.

> This world, indeed, is sacred; but, paradoxically, one cannot see the sacredness of the world until one discovers that it is a divine play. . . . One is devoured by Time, by History, not because one lives in them, but because one thinks them *real* and, in consequence, one forgets or undervalues eternity.[2]

Eliade's theme is congenial with the mind of Jesus. According to the Fourth Gospel, Jesus did not say that his disciples should be taken out of the world. To live in history is good. He did pray that they should not be of the world. "They are not of the world, even as I am not of the world" (John 17:16). To be of the world is to be absolutely dependent upon it, to live by its life force and to die when it withdraws that power, to be devoured by time and history, and to believe that time and history are singularly and ultimately the only reality. This depreciates new birth and resurrection. We can appreciate the world's sacredness only by realizing that it is a divine play. Otherwise, we are so impressed with its grim reality, its history that grinds us down, that we make death a synonym for nothingness.

The divine play concerning history is the responsibility of the church. It must provide the stage, the script, and the actors. Eliade's additional observations are vividly illustrative. Referring to modern man's equation between death and nothingness, Eliade makes a most significant distinction:

> Let us note, in a brief parenthesis, that when we speak of "modern man," his crises and anxieties, we are thinking primarily of one who has no faith, who is no longer in any living attachment to Judaeo-Christianity. To a believer, the problem of Death presents itself in other terms: for him, too, Death is a rite of passage. But a great part of the modern world has lost its faith, and for this mass of mankind anxiety in the face of Death presents itself as anguish before Nothingness.[3]

Apart from the Judeo-Christian faith, modern man has become the victim of history and its marriage to secularism. He is conscious of the end of himself because of his passion for history. That end is nothingness because of his passion for secularism. Is there any wonder that there is a frantic quality to his endeavor at doing good works? Does he not make a shambles of his ethical ventures because he is convinced that everything that is going to happen must happen here and now? Does he not stumble over his own feet in his harried haste to make his life count for something?

As a dramatizing presence, the church alone is qualified for reenacting the birth, life, death, and resurrection of Jesus Christ. This is its antidote for despair in an exceptionally historicized and secularized setting. For however long the church does this, dramatically and faithfully, the world will do well to see that the show goes on. Man might rightfully pray for the good of any setting in which the house of the Lord is allowed to put on its show.

ATTENTION TO LITURGY

All that is being said these days about the recovery of liturgy and the necessity for new and imaginative forms is extremely pertinent to the responsibility of the church for meaningful drama. Theater should have a place for the traditional and the contemporary, for Shakespeare and Albee. A similar span is appropriate for the church as far as traditional and contemporary liturgy is concerned.

Since liturgy is not within my competence, I cannot speak to its needs in highly specific ways. I am convinced that every segment of the church needs to take the matter of liturgy's recovery and modification quite seriously. Churches which have always been dependent upon liturgical worship should be in the forefront of the movement to greater imagination and communication. Sectarian groups, barren in liturgical history, need to join this movement. The time has passed when personal devotion and family prayers were sufficient for preparing people to worship in symbolically impoverished halls and in corporate worship without liturgical quickening and imagination. There may have been a time when the biblical word was devoured by those hungering and thirsting for righteousness. When these people gathered for worship, their appetites had already been whetted for the "bread of life." But those days are gone. Personal devotion and family worship are out of fashion and out of practice. The quality of worship has suffered accordingly.

Langdon Gilkey's question to a Quaker is germane. Gilkey had been a guest preacher at a Quaker meeting and wondered aloud about noticeable changes in their worship practices. They had an ordered service, sang hymns, and paid their minister for his sermons. The Quaker responded:

> I was raised a Quaker in a Quaker family, and grew up surrounded by a Quaker community—and the Inner Light spoke to all of us at the meetings we had together. But when we moved here to Poughkeepsie, and I began to sell stocks and bonds, all I could think of in that silence was the Dow-Jones stock averages—and so we wanted to have people who didn't think only of the market all week long to talk to us about religion.[4]

One does not have to be a Quaker to know what the man was talking about. All of us: plumbers, doctors, and cosmeticians need religious services which are dramatic events. If they are not, our worship experiences will not be as fulfilling as we must want them to be.

ON KNOWING THE SCRIPT

A good script is necessary for a good show. The church has a great script. It is too bad that so many of its actors have not bothered to master it. They should know the script. They must. It is the gospel. It is good news. It is proclamation that Jesus has come and has brought the kingdom near at hand. By his life, death, and resurrection all men may be saved. God's grace is effectively at work in the whole of creation. And in the Parousia the best is yet to be. With such a script for its base, the Scripture plays an endless symphony of faith, hope, and love; of response, obligation, affirmation, and promise.

Because the Redeemer has come and the Word became flesh, you have been given the power to become children of God. God so loved the world that he gave his only Son. Men who walked in darkness have seen a great light. All things work together for good with those who love God and are called according to his purpose. Nothing can separate us from the love of God. Whoever believes in Him shall not perish but have everlasting life. Give us our daily bread. Lead us not into temptation but deliver us from evil. Go home, prodigal. Hurry! Everyone except the elder brother and the fatted calf will be more than glad to see you.

Love God and love your neighbor. Love your enemy. Give him more cheek than he bargained for. Go two miles. Feed the hungry. Water the thirsty. Clothe the naked. Minister to the sick. Don't be afraid to go to prison to visit a friend or someone who needs a friend. Become all things to all men in order to save some. Become Jew, Greek, barbarian, Negro, Russian, Chinese, rich, poor, wise, or foolish for the sake of others. Love one another as Christ has loved you.

Tear up the roof if you have a friend who needs Jesus. Climb a tree to see him for yourself. Trim your lamps and save your oil; the bridegroom is on the way.

Shout hosanna and let go with the palms. You can't afford to miss the Last Supper. Don't count Judas out. The grace of God is wonderfully strange. Don't be too hard on Simon Peter. You may have done the same thing. Gethsemane is not for sleeping but for praying.

If we have been baptized with Jesus in a death like his, will we not also rise with him in a resurrection like his? I thirst. Father, forgive them. You will be with me in paradise. It is finished. Into your hands I give my Spirit.

Let's go back to fishing. We should not leave without paying our last respects. The tomb is empty! He is not here! Don't ask me; ask that angel. He is risen!!

We shall not all sleep, but we shall all be raised. O death, where is thy sting? O grave, where is your victory?

And I saw a new heaven and a new earth. . . .

Such is the script for Christians. Why then does the church prattle petty moralisms, which are no more effective than Eve's leaf? It teaches ten ways to tithe and forgets that people will pay for a good show. It worries about the Jesus people just the way it would have worried about John the Baptist, a strange and not quite respectable man. Its most comforting words are about good people rather than the redeeming Lord. Of course the church tries to be relevant. If it would follow the script, it would be relevant without trying.

THE IMPORTANCE OF CASTING

Casting the right people in the right roles is indispensable to a good show. The church cannot here ignore what is fundamental to the theater. God's redemptive care for all kinds of people cannot be dramatized unless all kinds of people are in the church.

The situation calls for active recruitment of such people rather than merely being receptive to those who seek out the church. The success of any drama depends in large measure upon the ability of the director to find the right people for the right part. Although auditions sometimes uncover exceptional talent which will fit the part, the successful director actively solicits the services of particular people for roles he has in mind.

In this wise the minister must assume the role of director in the theater of salvation. His task will be enormously difficult. It will not be enough for him to bring his local congregation to the point of accepting all kinds of people. He must convince them that it is his task to recruit them in persistently vigorous ways. He will be unbelievably successful if he is able to develop talent scouts in his congregation, who will help him with his recruitment.

As it now stands, the average congregation wants very much to enlist the "right kind of people." What that means as over against what I am trying to say is a decided contrast.

What is meant by the right kind of people has to do with propriety and respectability. The choices are made along the lines of class, color, and economics. Churchmen do not mind God's rather indiscriminate redemption of all species of people as long as he does not expect every one of his churches to be equally indiscriminate. No church can effectively be a theater of salvation as long as it is governed by this kind of mentality.

One of the most stirring and telling parables attributed to Jesus describes an invitation to a banquet. When the right kind of people who had been invited found reasons not to attend, the host was very provoked. He sent his servants into the whole community with an urgent request to fill his table with all kinds of people. Nothing better could happen to the church and thus to the world.

Rudolf Bultmann's interpretation of the twilight laborers is likewise relevant. They were paid as much as those who had worked all day long. Bultmann does not agree that this is a parable primarily emphasizing the grace of God. The last hour workers were paid because they had fulfilled the contract that had been made with the manager of the vineyard. In Bultmann's view they were rewarded because they were obedient to the call they had received. Implicit in this narrative is also the fact that they responded to a definite need. The harvest had to be accomplished before night came when no man could work. They were the right people at the right time to do the job. In other words, they were properly cast in their responsible roles. And it is quite clear that they did not just show up on the scene. The owner of the vineyard went out and got them.

In the same kind of dogged and persistent manner, the church must look for the right people to do the right job at the right time. This is necessary to effective casting for the good show. This is an endeavor in which the church must not relent or slow down or draw back. It needs to complete its cast.

11. In Need of a Servant Church

Not until the church is the proper kind of institution acting out the redemptive role is it time to consider itself as a servant church. I cannot agree with Gibson Winter's narrow view: "In the churches today, ministry is usually taken to mean what a clergyman does in and for the religious organization. In the servant Church, ministry is servanthood within the world."[1] I take these to be extremely contrived polarities. Ministry is actually both servanthood within the church and the world. One sphere does not exclude the other. When the church extends its own community and lives its style in the world community, that is ministry. When it dramatizes redemption even on its own stage, that is ministry. In forthright and tangible service to the world the church is, of course, also performing a ministry.

The church will be a better servant if and when it realizes the limitations of this latter kind of ministry. The church serves a society which it cannot hope to perfect within the limits of history. Sometimes its most telling ministry is at those junctures where society finds it useful but will not or cannot adhere to its principles. In other words, the church must serve the world on the world's terms without expecting approval or reward.

> "Suppose one of you has a servant ploughing or minding sheep. When he comes back from the fields, will the master say, 'Come along at once and sit down'? Will he not rather say, 'Prepare my supper, fasten your belt, and then wait on me while I have my meal; you can have yours afterwards'? Is he grateful to the servant for carrying out his orders? So with you: when you have carried out all your orders, you should say, 'We are servants and deserve no credit, we have only done our duty'" (Luke 17:7-10, NEB).

This should put to rout all those ideas suggesting that the church can save itself only by becoming the world's servant. The servanthood of the church demands a tough-minded realism for its task. A current idealism suggests that the world will respond to unselfish service and respond with gratitude. The church had better not take that idealism too seriously. Whether in Isaiah or Philippians, the servant is exalted by God and not by the culture which he serves. Let the servant church heed that ancient wisdom. It should expect no great reward. It should anticipate no great response.

Nor can the church even be sure that serving the social aims of the world will hasten the kingdom's coming. It is servant, if at all, because it must minister to men who are totally unaware of the kingdom and its promise. The church serves the needs of society rather than its ambitions. It is servant primarily to those without faith because those without faith are perhaps the most needful and the most miserable of all men.

THE BANE OF RELEVANCE

The more popular critics claim that the church has failed at servanthood because of its penchant for irrelevance. Someone needs to tangle with those critics, but he had better beware of the tangent on which this kind of debate will take him. The discussion will probably deteriorate into arguments about relevance rather than servanthood. The bane of relevance is very much at hand. An irrelevant church is obviously not equipped for servanthood. Better said it is not equipped to serve the world the way the world may want to be served.

There are two kinds of servants and two kinds of services. One is the servant who fulfills needs as they are experienced and interpreted by the one needing the servant. In this instance the person in need also tells the servant what to do. He decides about the relevance of the servant because if the servant cannot or will not do as he is told, he is judged to be irrelevant.

The other kind of servant meets those needs which he determines to be genuine. In this instance the one in need is not the master of the servant. He is not in any position to tell the servant what to do. As a result he is not qualified to decide as to the relevance of the servant.

Gibson Winter has hinted at this and made us wish that he had taken more time to clarify it. He believes that "The servant Church appears as the expression of God's gracious presence and promise in the midst of secularism. . . . Amid the disunity and secularism of the city, the Church is the ministering servant of *judgment* [italics mine] and hope." [2]

As long as the church is a ministering servant of judgment, the world is in poor position to decide on the question of its relevance. This kind of servanthood is a far cry from the caricature of a domestic, doing menial and odd jobs at the employer's bidding. Quite to the contrary, the servant church judges man and his needs and serves him in that context.

The church ought to guard against a preoccupation with relevance. Relevance is far too ambiguous a term. It cannot qualify as a cardinal virtue in the church's ministry. At the very least, every decision to be relevant ought to be made in light of the source which demands it. Otherwise it will be a very short hop from relevance to relativity about everything under the sun.

To be relevant, as things now stand, is to respond to whatever critic calls the relevance of the church into question. If anyone wishes to sound like a religious expert, let him pontificate about the irrelevance of the religious institution. Too many churchmen, unfortunate enough to hear him, throw themselves at his feet in sackcloth and ashes begging the critic to give them a lesson in relevance.

If this is the way to be relevant, the church has shown a remarkable facility for it. The church has looked to its environment and conducted itself accordingly. It is currently bombarded with the notion that the church must become urbanized. Since it seems to be predominantly rural, suburban, and familial in nature and style, it is deemed to be irrelevant to urban needs. This argument has to take place in a very small room. Not that the criticism is inaccurate; it is very much to the point. But where did we get this kind of church? And how? It grew out of the church's uncanny knack for being relevant. It came out of urban Europe and England to rural America. By accommodating to that early culture, the church became rural, suburban, and familial. Relevance is frequently a very relative matter.

Harvey Cox, Stephen Rose, Gibson Winter, Howard Moody, and Malcolm Boyd are relevant. So are Norman Vincent Peale, W. A. Criswell, Fulton J. Sheen, and Billy Graham. They just happen to be relevant to different kinds of people in different states of mind. The same observation applies to Edmund Muskie, Spiro Agnew, George Wallace, John Lindsay, and Ronald Reagan. It all depends on who is calling the shots. But in the final analysis genuinely relevant public servants must be the determining factors as to what is germane and material. If they fail to do this, their relevance will bury them in acculturated anonymity.

William Hamilton is refreshingly honest about all this. He has become quite apathetic about the church's relevance. "The theologian, however," he assumes, "is neither despairing nor hopeful about the church. He is not interested, and he no longer has the energy or interest to answer ecclesiastical questions about What the Church Must Do to Revitalize Itself." [3]

I believe I can see the bulge from Hamilton's tongue in his cheek. No theologian can be disinterested in the church. At the same time, I identify with his exhausted feeling about the relevance question. If the church sacrifices its authority for the sake of relevance, it will never be a servant church; for it alone must decide on the redemptive needs of the world.

ON NOT KNOWING WHAT TO DO

Maybe the poor little church has become so relevant that it does not know what to do. It gives evidence of that, revolving on its own pedestal in a cluttered world, like a cleaning woman in a dirty kitchen not knowing where to begin. The church is impetuously determined to get involved, but it does not know how or where. This has made the church vulnerable to any and all forces which will take it "where the action is." Most social agencies are glad to use the churches for their chief resources of manpower. They are quick to enlist the religiously motivated in their causes. They know churchmen will be conscientious, diligent, and faithful. For the most part these are good causes in which churchmen ought to enlist. But let no activist clergyman salve his own conscience and that of his congregation by assuring the body that when a Christian is at work in the world, there also is the church. This is a cheap and unworthy tactic for convincing ourselves that the church is indeed a servant.

The church's preoccupation with involvement is not dissimilar to an early morning scene in almost any southern city on almost any day of the week. Clusters of men gather on a number of accustomed corners. They comprise stagnated pools of casual and unskilled labor. They wait for someone to come by and take them to odd jobs around the city. On good days many of them are employed. Other days are not so good. But in any event they are waiting for jobs in which they are told what to do. Since they cannot do a particular thing very well, they are willing to do anything, also not very well. They are waiting for the action. They want to get involved. If no one involves them, they loiter along the streets, or con some innocents in a pool parlor, or go home to wait for whatever dark festivities the night may have to offer.

So it seems to be with the church. It has been standing on life's corners waiting for the mayor or the labor leader or the chamber of commerce or the welfare department to use its services and to tell it what to do. This reminds me of all us oafs, filled with good intentions, pressing the remaining members of a bereaved family and saying: "If there is anything I can do, let me know. When you have a few minutes, think of something for me to do." Troubled people have no time for thinking of things others can do for them. Neither does a troubled world.

An honorable moratorium must be declared and extended on this practice. There should be no more meetings at which an outsider is asked to come and tell the church what it ought to do in the world. If the church does not know what to do, there is no chance that the world can be of help in this cause. In the interim let the church simply bless the world by its presence. It should not bother the world with the demand for ideas by which it hopes to justify that presence.

THE CONFESSION OF A CLERGYMAN

To be sure, the church has failed to be servant because it has sometimes lacked the will. But there is no way to gauge its lack of will as long as it does not know how to be servant. After thirty years in the ministry, I must confess that the one reality which has burdened me the most, has frustrated me to the point of despair, and has given me an embittered view of my own profession has been my inability to move the church, as the church, into a world of need. God acts in the whole of history. God wants the church at work in the whole of history, but as the servant church. If the church has no peculiar service to render, indigenous to its faith, shape, and practice; there is no need to talk of a servant church. It would be more honest for the church to admit that it can do nothing whatsoever for the world.

Unfortunately, this incompetence on the part of clergy, which must be distinguished from the failure of laymen, has been insidiously camouflaged. This is true to the extent that a church may anticipate the outcome if it fires its preacher for incompetence. He will immediately find a social issue which he claims to have championed and will insist that this is the real reason for his dismissal. It is quite true that most congregations are unhappy at one time or another with social prophets in their pulpits as well as out in the community. It is quite true that some men have lost their pulpits as a result. But it is more frequently true that ministers are asked to leave because of their general incompetence. When this is the case, it does no service to the Christian cause to insist to the contrary. The time has come for clergymen to admit to this evasion and to confront each other because of it. After all, the difference between a prophet who is incompetent and one who is competent is a very big difference. Churches may wish to be rid of the latter just as much as the first, but they will have a more difficult time expediting that wish.

AT JUNCTURES OF THE ABSURD

The foregoing confession is not one having to do with irrelevance. A far more distressing cause lies behind the church's inability to serve the world. The church can do little or nothing at the junctures of the absurd. These are appearing with increasing frequency in current society. Life is without meaning in that arena. It is ridiculous. Under that circumstance people have no ear for judgment and no recognizable needs to be served.

In *A Rumor of Angels,* Peter Berger searches for *"signals of transcendence* within the empirically given human situation." [4] Finding them as reflections of human response instead of from the perspective of a "divine sender" will substantiate the reality of a religious dimension within our culture. Berger believes that one of these "signals of transcendence" is what he calls the *"argument from damnation."*

There are certain deeds that cry out to heaven. These deeds are not only an outrage to our moral sense, they seem to violate a fundamental awareness of the constitution of our humanity. In this way, these deeds are not only evil, but *monstrously evil*.[5]

If a sense of damnation is indeed one "signal of transcendence" for these times, it is a signal in danger of losing its clarity and its power. Were it not for the world's youth, the "argument from damnation" would hardly pertain. Youth are almost the only ones who still maintain their list of intolerables. Deeds that ought to "cry out to heaven" no longer raise that outcry in a number of instances. When men are silent rather than crying to heaven, when their "fundamental awareness of the constitution of our humanity" no longer recognizes when violation occurs, absurdity is more than a distant drummer. Its din is so close that we can hear nothing other than its dissonant notes of incongruity.

At the time of this writing, a recent massacre at New York State's Attica Prison had just left its bloody blemish on our history. The death toll of prisoners and the guards they were holding as hostages totaled forty or more. They were killed by a collection of troops which recaptured "cell block D" for the cause of law and order.

Attica was an absurdity. I shudder at having to say that I know of little or nothing that the church could have said or can say to or about that Attica event. It seems to have been unavoidable although predictable. We knew that it was going to happen somewhere. If my sense of the social pulse was accurate, we were not shocked. We were depressed but not shocked. No one cried to heaven. No one seemed to think that there was anything that God himself could do about Attica, much less the church.

If it were not for the fact that Attica's complete absurdity was foreshadowed in the biblical myth of Cain and Abel — an embryonic and minor absurdity — I would be forced to conclude that the church has nothing more to say in the world at all. The two events share a common factor. Each tells of a victim who felt he was treated unjustly by a remote and super power. This super power was God in the biblical story. It was the creators and enforcers of the law in the Attica event. In each instance the victim of injustice did not or could not deal with his oppressor. He withdrew from that confrontation. He became apathetic before the super power because he believed that his oppressor had no regard for him.

Rollo May has written of the consequences of apathy in this context.

> When inward life dries up, when feeling decreases and apathy increases, when one cannot affect or even genuinely *touch* another person, violence flares up as a daimonic necessity for contact, a mad drive forcing touch in the most direct way possible. . . . To inflict pain and torture at least proves that one can affect somebody.[6]

Cain, therefore, touched Abel with violent murder. Apathetic before the decision of God, he killed his little brother. That was absurd. The prisoners of Attica touched their fellow inmates and their guards with the same kind of violence. This was completely absurd because both their hostages and they themselves fell before the bullets of the attacking troops. To turn upon our brothers and our peers when we are alienated from the powers above us is absurd.

The comparison can go no farther. The Cain and Abel incident had its options. Attica did not have the one it needed. Because the minor absurdity of Cain and Abel still appears in modern society, the church can speak to it. And in speaking to it, the chances for avoiding the total absurdity of Attica are enhanced.

The church can say to a modern Cain: "You could become an atheist." Injustice and evil, unexplained and unrelieved, have always been the grounds for disbelief. A person can wipe God out of his own history by the posture and practice of unbelief. He can murder God with his atheism. And the church must be willing to say that this is more to be desired than to kill one's brother.

Cain could have argued with God. The matter was between God and him. He could have insisted that God had no right to disregard his offering while favoring that of Abel. There was no guarantee that Cain would have liked the answers he got. Job did not like what he heard when he was arguing the question of justice with God. Jeremiah did not like the answer to his question "Why do the righteous perish and the wicked prosper?" But both learned some lessons from their encounters. At the very least they learned that God was in power and that he was responsible for the way the world turned. If Cain had seen nothing but God's muscle as a result of the encounter, that would have been better than killing Abel.

Cain could have entertained the idea that his sacrifice was unworthy. The Bible is silent on that question. Thus it leaves the possibility open. Or Cain might have tried again with the same or a different sacrifice. In a text that may be somewhat corrupt but nonetheless fraught with important implications, God said to Cain, "Why are you angry, and why has your countenance fallen? If you do well, will you not be accepted? And if you do not do well, sin is couching at the door; its desire is for you, but you must master it" (Genesis 4:6-7). The situation was still negotiable. God left the next move up to Cain. And in that next move he killed his brother.

To a lesser degree and in greater complexity these options were open to the prisoners at Attica. The most important option was not. Cain could have done nothing. He could have trusted God. The prisoners of Attica were too alienated from the religious situation for that to have been viable. Between God and their own destiny stood the forces of power and law. The prisoner could not trust those forces because they had no assurance that those forces would heed the will of God or could recognize it when revealed. Such is the difference between a minor and a major absurdity — the difference between the Cain-Abel episode and Attica.

The church must serve the world on religious terms. Through the Cain-Abel episode much may be said. Attica leaves nothing to be said. The church must realize this for itself and convince the world of it before it girds up its loins and goes forth to do service.

Attica confirmed the prophecy of Amos:

> "Behold, the days are coming," says the Lord God,
> "when I will send a famine on the land;
> not a famine of bread, nor a thirst for water,
> but of hearing the words of the Lord."
> Amos 8:11

God was silent at Attica. The church could not be otherwise.

This does not mean that the failure of the servant church is inevitable and irrevocable in our time. It means only that the church must be the church even when it serves the world. It must speak the word of God and do the service of God. When life reaches the juncture of the absurd, God will likely be silent. So must the church be silent.

Langdon Gilkey's book *How the Church Can Minister to the World Without Losing Itself* is significantly and ably done. I am able to recognize the church in his work, but I did not see its servanthood as clearly as I would like. On the other hand, Gibson Winter strongly identifies the servanthood of the church in *The New Creation as Metropolis*. In so doing he obscures the church until it is hard to identify.

The challenge is still upon us. The religious establishment must be the servant-church without suffering noticeable loss on either side of the hyphen. If this is impossible, it is time to find it out. The best of our thought and energy, coupled with great devotion, must be committed to the realization of that goal until and unless we discover that it is impossible.

12. The Servant Church

The major emphasis in this final chapter will be on the servant church as a religious institution. Such an emphasis will demand a more specific description of the work of the servant church than is usually the case. It will mean, among other things, that the church must stop taking undue credit for everything that Christians are doing for the good of society. The church has a right to take some credit. But it is not exclusively responsible for the ethical practices of its members in their work for social betterment.

The church has taken too much comfort at the sight of its members actively participating in the social, economic, and political structures of culture. Other persons, with little or no motivation from ecclesiastical forces, are equally hard at work in the same settings. Nor can the church claim exclusive credit for the theological perspectives from which social action is informed. Secularization has brought about what Martin Marty calls "religion in general." This assures the fact that there are many "secular theologians," who have adopted the principles of religious doctrine without being "religious" as far as connection with the church is concerned.

Such a clarification is not intended to disparage the participation of theologically informed people in every segment of society. It is simply to say that this goes on without overt participation by the church as a religious institution. There is no evidence that even those churchmen who engage society at these junctures do so because they are members of the church. They do so because they are human beings and concerned citizens. Let the church rejoice in and celebrate this reality without expecting merit badges for it.

Clergymen need to practice a particular integrity at this point. Their tendency to congratulate their congregations and themselves because the members are "involved" in the affairs of society is unfortunate. This congratulation usually allows the church in question to avoid the challenge of serving the world as an expression of the church. Every person should be encouraged to live prophetically in his time. He should certainly expect to be encouraged by his church in this respect. One cringes before the speculation of what kind of sorry world this would be if people were not inclined to care enough to pertain to the world around them. So long as that encouragement does not proceed to the next step of self-congratulation, the church is doing as it should. It must not, however, lose sight of what it can and must do as a Christian institution.

SANCTUARY

The church historically has been a sanctuary for those in need of refuge. It is uniquely "church" in this regard. The most dramatic and recent example unfolds around young men seeking sanctuary from the demands of the military. There are no legal sanctions against invading a religious sanctuary and taking draft dodgers or deserters into custody. Nor should the church ask for immunity in this regard. At the same time, ancient "cities of refuge" were set apart for good reason. They afforded relief from tyranny and from oppressive judgment. They were barriers against quick and unjust punishment by insensitive powers and authorities. Most specifically they protected persons, guilty of accidental homicide, from immediate and ruthless destruction.

The sanctuary afforded by the modern church is primarily

symbolic. It does not enjoy the same kind of lawful encouragement as its ancient prototypes. Its symbolic value is nonetheless important. Each time a conscientious objector or deserter takes refuge in the church, two vital issues are highlighted. The horror of war is accented. Whenever a young man is dragged by his heels from the altar because he does not want to kill, the conscience of the land is scratched and awakened. Then, too, the same principle holds if a person seeks sanctuary for reasons of cowardice rather than conscience. Even cowards need a place to go and to hide. Everyone needs some place to go when he cannot stand the world for whatever reason. Havens of mercy are all too rare in a day so slavishly committed, at least in word, to the principles of justice.

This is but to say that the church ought to be a sanctuary for all the world's untouchables. It can hardly be more prophetic than when it does this. Churches make a dramatic protest against a closed society when they are open to those whom society will not tolerate. Not only do the preachers need to sermonize on the church's openness to society's misfits, they must urge their congregations to open up their buildings. They will soon discover that the average congregation is more willing to be sermonized on the matter than to put it into practice. That is all the more reason to see that the doors are opened.

In the second place, there is much to commend the church as a sanctuary for the uprooted and the lonely. Let us first deal with the obvious. People are lonely and alienated by virtue of discrimination and poverty. No greater need for churchly sanctuary may be imagined than with reference to them. An open ministry to the rootless and estranged people of our society is a fundamental responsibility for the church.

The church ought to be a socializing agent in our culture. This means that it must be sanctuary to culture's polarities. The rich and the poor are lonely because they are polarized. This reality is enjoying more and more recognition. This is not all. "Middle America" may be suffering the most acute loneliness of all. The "silent majority" is not so much silent as it is invisible. Middle-class Americans are possibly the most invisible people of all. The worst ghetto has a high degree of visibility. Its inhabitants usually know one another. Its miserable spectacle intrudes upon the American vision. The very rich are also visible to each other. They make small colonies in their parts of the world. Each is alienated and needs sanctuary and reconciliation. On the other hand, the alienation of "middle Americans" is not so clearly delineated.

Their loneliness surfaces when they begin to make choices of churches in the towns and cities to which they have migrated. Those seeking churches are a microcosm of the whole pattern, which affords us a model for study. Numerous religious surveys have revealed that newcomers choose churches that are "warm and friendly." The ego of most clergymen is affronted by this fact. Preachers like to think that they are the chief reasons that people decide for one church against another. This is not the case and it should not be the case. No one needs more of the integrative and socializing ministry of churches than does the anonymous and lonely "middle American."

James Gustafson has recognized the possibilities of profound results in this context more than anyone else I know:

> The affirmation that God acts in history means that in his power and good pleasure he chooses to use that which can be interpreted without reference to him as a means of ruling and making himself known. . . .
> Thus the commonplace, e.g., the American rural Protestant church supper, can be a human gathering and occasion through which God can act and speak.[1]

This is just as appropriate for the mobile suburbanite as it is for the farmer. The practice started with rural people, not only as a theological symbol but as a means of overcoming their geographical distances from one another. The mobility of modern middle-class people has caused an equal degree of remoteness for them. Churches ought to hang on to their kitchens and their social halls. These are also places of reconciliation.

In the third place, the church must offer sanctuary for those who want to keep a sense of the sacred. This means that the religious edifice ought to be immediately recognizable as a church. It should serve as a "God-reminder" for everyone who sees it. It makes no difference whether the architecture is traditional or modern. What does count is that the servant church look like a church.

To whatever extent buildings enhance the face of the neighborhood let the church add its own radiance. I am moved by the church in the countryside keeping vigil over the farmer and reminding him that he is steward of the land. The church in the ghetto, sometimes an opulent incongruity, is an architectural and eschatological beatitude: "Blessed are the poor." It almost sings for its people: "When the Roll is Called up Yonder, I'll be There." I like upstart chapels on the campus — God's effigies hanging over mocking academe — badgering the "truth hounds" by proclaiming the truth they already know to those still thrashing around in the chase to run it down. I am fascinated by the church in the city littered with metropolitan trash and begrimed by urban filth. It wheezes out its stubborn word like an asthmatic old man who will not sell his priceless land to the most persuasive entrepreneurs. And whenever I see a church standing by unmarked crossroads, I have a sense of knowing the way.

Is this maudlin sentimentality? You will never get me to believe that. In a day that is measurably bereft of justice and love, judgment and mercy, hope and faith, the standing and visible church vividly interrupts both skyline and landscape with sacred meanings I cannot afford to lose and do not wish to forget.

MONEY

The church can serve the world in highly creative ways by the imaginative use of money. Both the secular idealists and the religious purists do not give due consideration to the possibilities of doing good through the medium of money.

Most of the books and articles on what the church must do in reshaping its mission to the present world say little or nothing about money. Those which do have something to say are mostly content with another polemic against the money wasted by the denominational hierarchies. Bureaucracy is just as much a dirty word in religious circles as it is in the general whirl of things.

Many congregations oversimplify the problem. They tend to think that the local parish is a much better and wiser steward than its denomination can ever hope to be. This is only a partial truth although a very important one. The parish church is more flexible in its approaches to the creative use of money. It is less bureaucratic. That is because its programs do not demand tenure to the same degree as do the long-range objectives of a denomination. In turn, however, denominations are geared to meet needs of a magnitude which would overwhelm the resources of any given church.

This dilemma cannot be quickly or easily resolved. There is one thing which could promise an eventual solution. Local churches ought to keep enough money to support their parish ministries, providing that such churches are interested in and capable of innovative and imaginative missions. They should not carry this to the extreme. Denominational missions that have passed the vital tests of time and experience deserve the continuing support of their participating churches.

On the other hand, the denominations must relate to their cooperating churches in good faith. Their present practice is to flinch defensively every time a church reduces its pledge to the denominational enterprise. It would be far better if denominations were willing to learn from the creative ministries of some of their churches. When a local church is doing something that is worthwhile, it deserves commendation and financial support from the denomination. Denominational leadership should be quick to encourage the churches to plow new ground by assessing them in less amounts for denominational work or by commending them when they reduce their contributions. In many cases the denomination ought to make outright gifts to those churches which are accomplishing meritorious results in their own local ministries. This recommendation must be distinguished from a practice that is already in operation. Denominations do make outright gifts to local churches. For the most part, however, these are churches which are presumably expediting the "innovative ministries" of their denominations. This is often no more than a camouflage of denominational business as usual. Churches ought to be set free and financially supported in order for them to persist in the missions which they have devised and are eager to carry on. Only then will the denomination eventually benefit from vigorous and fresh ideas of mission.

"Emergency assistance funds" immediately come to mind as a possible first example. Neither religious nor secular bureaucracies are structured for services of this nature. They operate on such large scales as to prohibit immediate actions for alleviating small but poignant crises. Local churches are able to respond to such emergencies. As close as each congregation is to its minister, it is able to give him discretionary powers with minimal risks. Many churches are already engaged in this ministry. Their funds are too small to do more than offer token aid as a general rule. They frequently solve this problem by direct solicitation of the congregation. This is better than nothing. A more effective solution would be a dramatic increase of this item in their budgets.

Emergency assistance calls for small amounts of money for frequent and various needs. It deals with food, clothing, eviction, fuel for cooking and warmth, alcoholism, medicine, and the like. No program of emergency assistance should be highly organized. Quick delivery of services is its peculiar genius. Considerable trust in the minister, and possibly a small committee, is necessary.

The bulk of emergency funds should probably remain

with the local church. This will assure greater discretion and immediate action. In some instances a council of local churches may be better suited for delivering some of the necessary services. Parishes, which cannot provide for emergencies within their own constituencies, could then be enabled to care for their own unfortunates.

Secular agencies need the help of churches in the realm of emergency assistance. Their guidelines for dispensing their own monies usually militate against quick action. At the same time, these agencies uncover needs which do not appear to the churches. Whenever those needs are in the nature of an emergency, the funds of the churches sometimes stand between the beneficiaries and tragic consequences. Every parish minister ought to have a "hot line" between secular charities and his own office.

The most exciting and encouraging stewardship, as far as a given congregation is concerned, is the use of "seed money" for innovative ministries. Emergency assistance must be mostly confidential in order to be effective. The congregation's left hand should be generally unaware of what its right hand is doing in this respect. However, "seed money" does not call for restrictions of confidentiality.

"Seed money" is designed to encourage persons, in the church or otherwise, to give their time and talents to social and personal needs in any given community. These missions need not always be "religious" in the strictest sense of the word. A continuing conversation between the ministering unit and the sponsoring church, however, is fundamental to such ventures.

This kind of work constitutes a gift of money by the church to individuals or groups which are willing to participate personally in mission to the community. Many such ministries demand a comparatively small amount of money and may be supported by congregations with no more than average resources. The essence of the endeavor is one of ingenuity and imagination by which inauspicious but meritorious needs are uncovered and met.

The church I serve has invested some money which produced initially the modest amount of around $2,000 per year. By using these funds wisely, we have initiated and sustained — with the help of other churches — a "meals on wheels" ministry. This service delivers two meals, five days a week, to aging, indigent, and convalescent persons who would need institutional care were it not for this ministry. We have supported student groups working with children in transitional and blighted areas. We have helped to set up a recruitment center for the purpose of introducing university students to community services of many kinds. An ongoing food bank for the poor, a revolving fund to be used by the local police in emergency assistance, support and participation in one or more day-care centers, and tutoring in a number of schools have also been initiated or supported, wholly or in part, as a result of our own "seed money" philosophy and projects. Fundamental to all of these endeavors is the fact that those seeking financial assistance for their missions are also actively and consistently engaged in them.

Stewardship in the role of Christian advocacy may be the wave of the future. The church has left this category virtually untouched up until now. That major charity is beyond the means of churches is clearly evident. A pool of mission money, raised by all the churches in this country, could not eliminate poverty from a single medium-size city in the United States. It might not be enough even to rid the ghettos of rats. Direct gifts to the poor are dramatic acts. Their effectiveness is another matter. Some churches are constructing low-rent housing units for underprivileged people. Such endeavors are worthwhile as modular reminders of the housing problems of the poor. They miss the mark, on the other hand, if they represent religious assumptions that the church is going to solve the nation's housing problems out of its own resources.

A more rewarding ministry in the long run could be the church's advocacy to the centers of power and affluence on behalf of the powerless and the poor. This would mean that the church would confront the very people who often contribute to the plight of the unfortunate. Landlords and real estate officers, lawyers, doctors, professional figures, businessmen, and politicians populate the membership of churches. Let the church directly confront them as advocate. This will mean that local parishes will provide expenses for powerful prophets of worthwhile causes to confront their own constituencies. Money that purchases the various media for the sake of alerting society to the needs of the poor is more effective than money given in direct gifts to the indigent masses.

A study of the history of stewardship startlingly reveals the one-track mind of the church in this regard. It has used the bulk of its money in priestly practices. It has almost exclusively ministered directly to the victims of any given culture. This eventuality is other than mere happenstance. New Testament Scriptures in particular have encouraged the priestly use of money. They have encouraged giving to the poor almost without exception.

The Gospel's account of the woman who anointed Jesus is illustrative. The disciples wondered why this expensive ointment was not put to better use. It could have been sold and the proceeds distributed among the poor. In such primitive times, poverty was not fraught with the complexities that now are the case. Then, too, the strong eschatological strain in the New Testament militated against well-devised programs against poverty. New Testament people did not believe that the world would last long enough to justify anti-poverty campaigns. Under those circumstances, simple and uncomplicated charity was the most sensible course to follow.

This situation no longer prevails. Poverty is entrenched in highly complex ways. Eschatological theology is no longer viewed in terms of calendar time. The world may be with us for a very long time. All of this demands the use of a Christian's money in prophetic ways. The steward must learn to be prophet as well as priest. He may even need to be more prophet than priest as things now stand. The use of its money in the role of an advocate is one of the church's best chances for being prophetic on the modern scene.

CLERGY

In order to practice its servanthood, the church must cool the current passion for "lay ministry." The church's failure to be a proper servant suggests a crisis in the clergy and not among the laymen.

This contention is not in violation of the doctrine of the "priesthood of believers." That dogma originated in the assertion that men needed no priestly mediators between God and themselves. Everyone was competent for communion with God as the result of the grace of God. The focus was on an individual's relationship with God rather than on his relationship to other men. The doctrine of universal priesthood remains a grand document in this sense and is essential to the dignity of men.

A question for present consideration concentrates on the "priesthood of believers" as it refers to "person to person" relationships instead of "person to God" relationships. Are laymen better equipped to be priests and prophets to other laymen than are clergymen? Are laymen more able to assure the servanthood of the religious institution than are clergymen? These are the questions which clamor for answers if there is to be a servant church. I must say that I believe clergymen are more indispensable to these endeavors than are laymen. My answer is almost entirely determined by my view of the clergyman as a professional.

I say this to the fact of the persistent contention that the clergy is already much too professional. It is assumed that making one's livelihood from ministry is an offense to the truly spiritual. Perhaps it is better to say that this was the argument's gist in former years. Integrity and conviction are synonyms for the same doubt in present times.

Of more serious import is the assumption that the clergy

could or would be more prophetic if its livelihood were not tied to congregational support. No honest clergyman will contend that he never has given a second thought to his salary when embroiled in controversial and unpopular causes. In fact, we clergymen sometimes never get as far as the second thought. The first symptom of resistance sends us scurrying to see if Elijah has room for us in his cave. On the other hand, no other arrangement could attest to a preacher's conviction as much as that of laying his job on the line. People have to give some notice to what he says or does when he risks the security of his family for the sake of his convictions.

Clergymen would not necessarily be more courageous under other circumstances. Timid prophets can always find good enough reasons for flinching. Their opponents would be ingenious enough to contrive other threats. There are just as many ways of getting at the man as there are of getting to his money. All kinds of prophets must take their risks and their lumps. Both politicians and labor organizers know the meaning of fear.

If preachers are human — and I think they really are — they will experience the heights of courage and the depths of fear as do average men. Whether or not they are paid, preachers face ostracism, loss of approval, rifts with friends, and many other reasons for forebodingness. In the final analysis, a clergyman who is not paid is simply not paid.

Placing renewed importance upon the role of the clergyman may reintroduce the ecclesiastical double standard to society. The sooner the better is an appropriate response to the possibility. Let both the personal and professional categories of the clergy be embraced in that double standard. There should be no sharp distinction between the two.

The bond between person and profession is nowhere more explicit and exacting than with the clergy. The fact that Paul made his living as a tentmaker is frequently invoked by those wishing to eliminate a professional clergy. They attach more significance to this matter than did the biblical writers.

No importance was attached to the possibility that Jesus did some secular work. Mark's reference "Is not this the carpenter . . ." (Mark 6:3) is generally thought to be an edition of the text. In any event, it may be concluded that Jesus' major task was proclaiming the gospel when he embarked on his public ministry. His livelihood, personhood, and mission were all of a piece.

Instead of being less so, the professional clergyman *ought to be a better Christian* than are the average members of his parish. He should demand this of himself, and the congregation has a right to expect it of him. This does not mean that he is necessarily a better person. It does mean that, because of his work, the clergyman ought to be more intense and intent in terms of his Christianity. He cannot afford the luxury of moods, as laymen can, in order to explain an absence of compassion. He must always be concerned for troubled, hurt, lost, and grieving people. No matter how much he is burdened with his own personal problems, he is conditioned and trained to shoulder the burdens of others. Like Ezekiel, who lost his wife at evening time, the clergyman must rise in the morning to do the Lord's commands. The preacher is expected to confront the bigot and to live out a work of reconciliation no matter how deep and wide his own prejudices may be. These are the responsibilities of every Christian. There can be no question about that. But these are the responsibilities at which the minister works night and day to a degree unmatched by any other person.

The clergyman should be more alert to the primary miracles of his time. Modern man tends to shy away from primary miracles and possibly settle for subordinate ones. J. G. Hamann's reflections on John 12:29f. are apt:

> "The crowd standing by heard the voice and said that it had thundered. Others said, An angel has spoken to him."
>
> How the slightest circumstances are prophetic in Holy Scriptures! Here we see human reason straying in two ways, which have persisted to our own time: explaining the voice of God by natural effects or by subordinate miracles. Rather than see and believe God, men imagine thunder or an angel. At the same time this is the effect which the revelation of God would have upon sinners and pious people. The unbeliever will hear a

thunderclap, when the believer and the Christian hears angels' voices speaking to him.²

Every burning bush may be that primary miracle, and no clergyman can afford to take the chance of passing it by. He has to see if there is fire in the smoke. He tries to hear the voice of God in riots, wars, parties, and politics. When the morticians of radical theology post the funeral services of God, the preacher has to be there. As it turns out, he pays his last respects to the theologians and follows a living God back into the "herky-jerky" of life.

By virtue of his profession, the clergyman acquires a richness of experience not available to everyone; at least he should. He can reap the harvest of abundant experience from the endless variety of his mission. He lives with people across the entire range of the human saga, from birth to death. His life is a banquet of diversity. What a pity that many of us are somehow starving to death!

The recovery of the ecclesiastical double standard will bring the minister's calling back into focus. The idea that every man is called to be a minister, no matter what the nature of his trade or profession, has been in vogue for some time. This ground was dearly won. It should not be relinquished without a fight. That eventuality makes one hesitate to suggest a new look at the minister's calling. With all due regard for the risks involved, it must be argued that the call to be a professional minister is not synonymous with the call to minister through some other medium. The professor is a seeker. The preacher is a proclaimer. A professor does well to encourage his students to seek out every truth by means of rigid and objective analysis. The preacher relies on the assumption of truth as an *a priori* before analysis is in order. The professor believes what he knows in his profession. The preacher knows what he believes in his profession. A professor is tentative. A preacher must be convincing.

So it is that the man and the institution are inseparable if either is to be servant. The preacher and the church are inseparable if either is to be servant. Some years back H. Richard Niebuhr suggested that theological education prepared students for almost every task other than administering a "church as church" in modern society. I remember vaguely agreeing with his estimate of theological education. It has taken much longer for me to appreciate his argument with respect to its basic motif. Niebuhr claimed that the modern clergyman should

> . . . think of himself neither as parish parson responsible for all the people in a geographic area nor as the abbot of a convent of the saved, but only as the responsible leader of a parish church; it is the Church, not he in the first place, that has a parish and responsibility for it.[3]

To see that the church does its mission is the main task for the clergyman. This idea has gone out of style. It may never have been in style in the present era. Today's clergy tends to believe in its personal mission to the parish. There are more and more sounds to the effect that preachers can do better without the church. These clergymen see the church as an encumbrance to their personal mission. This goes Jesus one better in the decision to do mission all by oneself. Jesus apparently felt the need for a few disciples. He even organized them to the extent of appointing a treasurer.

Niebuhr's argument made little impact. His suggestion that the minister should be a *pastoral director* may have been a major reason. That has no more spiritual appeal than family movies have sex appeal. I rejected that label when first I read it. I did not like the image that it indicated. It left the office of clergy with connotations neither holy nor wise.

I am now more than eager to admit my mistake in rejecting Niebuhr's perceptive wisdom. It is the church, rather than the parson, which has a parish and is responsible for it. The church will hardly become servant unless and until preachers know again the exhilaration of directing churches to genuine mission in the world. And this may just be the key to the preacher's rediscovery of the excitement and effectiveness in his work.

Who knows? There may come to pass another era in which clergymen no longer hate the church. Once more, perhaps on that day between the third day of resurrection and the last day of *Parousia,* which the church has called the Lord's, the faithful community will joyfully dramatize the redemptive love of God. Who knows? Clergymen may once again go gladly on the Lord's Day to proclaim that Jesus is the Christ.

Notes

CHAPTER 1
[1] Rudolf Bultmann, "Preaching: Genuine and Secularized," *Religion and Culture: Essays in Honor of Paul Tillich*, ed. Walter Leibrecht (New York: Harper & Row, Publishers, 1959), p. 237.
[2] Carl Gustavson, *The Institutional Drive: A Study in Pluralistic Democracy* (Athens, Ohio: Ohio University Press, 1966), p. 113.
[3] Jerome H. Skolnick and Elliot Currie, eds., *Crisis in American Institutions* (Boston: Little, Brown and Company, 1970), pp. 14-15.

CHAPTER 2
[1] Theodore Roszak, *The Making of a Counter Culture* (Garden City, N.Y.: Doubleday & Company, Inc., 1969), p. 31.
[2] *Ibid.*, p. 26.
[3] Reinhold Niebuhr, *The Nature and Destiny of Man* (New York: Charles Scribner's Sons, 1947), p. 61.
[4] Kenneth Cauthen, "The Case for Christian Biopolitics," *The Christian Century*, November 19, 1969, p. 1481. Reprinted by permission of the Christian Century Foundation.

CHAPTER 3
[1] Rollo May, *Love and Will* (New York: W. W. Norton & Company, Inc., 1969), p. 49.
[2] *Ibid.*, pp. 41-42.
[3] Langdon Gilkey, *Maker of Heaven and Earth: A Study of the Christian Doctrine of Creation* (Garden City, N.Y.: Doubleday & Company, Inc., 1959), p. 51.
[4] *Ibid.*, pp. 49-50.

CHAPTER 4
[1] Roger Lincoln Shinn, *Man: The New Humanism*, vol. 6, from *New Directions in Theology Today*, ed. William Hordern (Philadelphia: The Westminster Press, 1968), p. 24. Used by permission.
[2] *Ibid.*, p. 170.

[3] Erich Fromm, *The Heart of Man: Its Genius for Good and Evil* (New York: Harper & Row, Publishers, 1964), p. 88.
[4] *Ibid.*, p. 91.
[5] Marshall McLuhan, *Understanding Media: The Extensions of Man* (New York: McGraw-Hill Book Company, 1964), p. 51.
[6] Kahlil Gibran, *The Prophet* (New York: Alfred A. Knopf, Inc., 1923), p. 15.

CHAPTER 5
[1] Peter L. Berger, *The Noise of Solemn Assemblies* (Garden City, N.Y.: Doubleday & Company, Inc., 1961), p. 123.
[2] Paul Tillich, *The Protestant Era* (Chicago: The University of Chicago Press, 1948), p. 226.
[3] Eberhard Jüngel, "God—As a Word of Our Language," *Theology of the Liberating Word*, ed. Frederick Herzog, trans. Robert Osborne (Nashville: Abingdon Press, 1971), p. 38.
[4] Horton Davies, *Worship and Theology in England: From Watts and Wesley to Maurice, 1690-1850* (Princeton, N.J.: Princeton University Press, 1961), vol. 3, pp. 124-125. Reprinted by permission of Princeton University Press and Oxford University Press.
[5] Jüngel, *op. cit.*, p. 36.
[6] Jaroslav Pelikan, *Spirit Versus Structure: Luther and the Institutions of the Church* (New York: Harper & Row, Publishers, 1968), p. 31.

CHAPTER 6
[1] Rollo May, *Love and Will* (New York: W. W. Norton & Company, Inc., 1969), p. 230.
[2] Peter L. Berger, *The Sacred Canopy* (Garden City, N.Y.: Doubleday & Company, Inc., 1967), pp. 39, 23.
[3] *Ibid.*, pp. 3-4.
[4] William Barclay, *The Mind of St. Paul* (New York: Harper & Row, Publishers, 1958), p. 121.
[5] Martin Dibelius, *Paul*, edited and completed by Werner Georg Kümmel, trans. Frank Clarke (Published in the United States of America in Philadelphia: The Westminster Press, 1953), pp. 107-108. Used by permission.
[6] B. F. Skinner, *Contingencies of Reinforcement: A Theoretical Analysis* (New York: Appleton-Century-Crofts, 1969 and 1972 [Paperback ed.], pp. 272, 284. By permission of Appleton-Century-Crofts, Educational Division, Meredith Corporation.
[7] *Ibid.*, p. 60.

CHAPTER 7
[1] Franklin H. Littell, *The Anabaptist View of the Church: A Study in the Origin of Sectarian Protestantism* (Boston: Beacon Press, 1958), pp. 65-66.
[2] Alec R. Vidler, *20th Century Defenders of the Faith* (Published in the United States of America in New York: The Seabury Press, Inc., 1965), pp. 121-122. Reprinted with permission. Published in England by SCM Press, Ltd.
[3] Peter L. Berger, "The Relevance Bit Comes to Canada," *The Restless Church*, ed. William Kilbourn (New York: J. B. Lippincott Co., 1966), pp. 78-79. Copyright © 1966 by McClelland and Stewart Limited. Reprinted by permission of The Canadian Publishers, McClelland and Stewart Limited, Toronto, and J. B. Lippincott Company.

144 • AT THE RISK OF IDOLATRY

⁴ D. M. Baillie, *God Was in Christ* (New York: Charles Scribner's Sons, 1948), p. 96.
⁵ Neville Clark, *Interpreting the Resurrection* (Published in the U.S.A. in Philadelphia: The Westminster Press, 1967), p. 65. Copyright © SCM Press Ltd., 1967. Used by permission.
⁶ *Ibid.*, p. 65.
⁷ *Ibid.*, p. 75.

CHAPTER 8
¹ Karl Barth, *Church Dogmatics, The Doctrine of Creation*, trans. Knight, Bromiley, Reid, and Fuller (Edinburgh: T. & T. Clark, 1960), vol. 3, part 2, p. 283.
² *Ibid.*, p. 284.
³ Paul Tillich, *Systematic Theology* (Chicago: University of Chicago Press, 1963), vol. 3, pp. 174-175.

CHAPTER 9
¹ Stephen C. Rose, ed., *Who's Killing the Church?* (New York: Association Press, 1966), p. 89.

CHAPTER 10
¹ Mircea Eliade, *Myths, Dreams and Mysteries*, trans. Phillip Mairet (New York: Harper & Row, Publishers, 1960), p. 30.
² *Ibid.*, p. 242.
³ *Ibid.*, p. 236.
⁴ Langdon Gilkey, *How the Church Can Minister to the World Without Losing Itself* (New York: Harper & Row, Publishers, 1964), p. 111.

CHAPTER 11
¹ Gibson Winter, *The New Creation as Metropolis* (New York: The Macmillan Company, 1963), pp. 58-59. Copyright © Gibson Winter, 1963.
² *Ibid.*, p. 54.
³ Thomas J. J. Altizer and William Hamilton, *Radical Theology and the Death of God* (Indianapolis: The Bobbs-Merrill Co., Inc., 1966), p. 88.
⁴ Peter L. Berger, *A Rumor of Angels* (Garden City, N.Y.: Doubleday & Company, Inc., 1969), p. 65.
⁵ *Ibid.*, p. 82.
⁶ Rollo May, *Love and Will* (New York: W. W. Norton & Company, Inc., 1969), pp. 30-31.

CHAPTER 12
¹ James M. Gustafson, *Treasure in Earthern Vessels: The Church as a Human Community* (New York: Harper & Row, Publishers, 1961), pp. 108-109.
² Ronald Gregor Smith, *J. G. Hamann: A Study in Christian Existence* (New York: Harper & Row, Publishers, 1960), p. 134.
³ H. Richard Niebuhr, *The Purpose of the Church and Its Ministry* (New York: Harper & Row, Publishers, 1956), p. 91.